Rocky Mountain National Park Road Guide

THE ESSENTIAL GUIDE FOR MOTORISTS

by
Thomas Schmidt

NATIONAL GEOGRAPHIC
WASHINGTON, D.C.

Contents

"We had a distant view of the summit of a range of mountains—which to our great satisfaction and heart felt joy, was declared by the commanding officer to be the range of the Rocky Mountains . . . a high Peake was plainly to be distinguished towering above all the others as far as the sight extended."

Today they'd be wearing spandex. Though fashions have changed, the view from the summit of Eagle Cliff is much the same.

> —Capt. John. R. Bell, 1820, describing
> the Front Range and the peak soon named
> after his commander, Maj. Stephen H. Long

"No words can describe our surprise, wonder and joy at beholding such an unexpected sight."

> —Milton Estes on his first view
> of Estes Park, 1859

"The air is scented with the sweet-smelling sap of the pines, whose branches welcome many feathered visitors from southern climes; an occasional humming-bird whirrs among the shrubs, trout leap in the creeks, insects buzz in the air; all nature is active and exuberant with life."

> —Windham Thomas Wyndham-Quin,
> Fourth Earl of Dunraven,
> who first visited Estes Park in 1872

"Go to the trees and get their good tidings. Have an autumn day in the woods, and beneath the airy arches of limbs and leaves linger in the paths of peace."

> —Enos Mills

"On top of the Ridge, the wind birrs across, swooping up from the deep dark green valley below. There is something about an alpine wind: it can blear the eyes and chill the fingers and be exceedingly irksome, but it seems to come from the back of beyond…"

> —On Trail Ridge, from Land Above the Trees,
> by Ann Zwinger and Beatrice Willard

How to Use This Guide

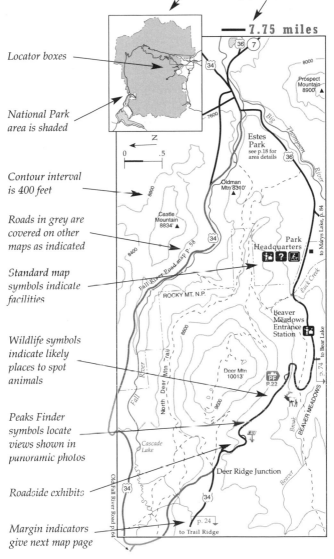

Locator maps show location and coverage of main maps

Mileage for highlighted road

Locator boxes

National Park area is shaded

Contour interval is 400 feet

Roads in grey are covered on other maps as indicated

Standard map symbols indicate facilities

Wildlife symbols indicate likely places to spot animals

Peaks Finder symbols locate views shown in panoramic photos

Roadside exhibits

Margin indicators give next map page

7.75 miles

Prospect Mountain 8900'

Estes Park
see p.18 for area details

Oldman Mtn 8310'

Castle Mountain 8834'

Park Headquarters

ROCKY MT. N.P.

Beaver Meadows Entrance Station

Deer Mtn 10013'

Cascade Lake

Deer Ridge Junction

to Marys Lake, p. 84

to Bear Lake

BEAVER MEADOWS

p. 24
to Trail Ridge

Fall River Road, map p. 58

Old Fall River Road p.64

- Key maps inside front cover give page numbers for road maps.

- Map features and commentary run side by side.

- Maps generally in sequence. Page numbers for adjoining maps are given in map margins. Or refer to locator maps or key maps.

- This book is a guide for motorists, not hikers or other backcountry users, who will find topographic maps and trail guides essential.

A Land Lifted
High Above the Trees

RENOWNED FOR ITS HIGH, glacially carved peaks and
its magnificent sprawl of alpine tundra, Rocky
Mountain National Park straddles the Continental
Divide sixty miles northwest of Denver. The park
embraces 415 square miles along the Front Range and
includes more than a hundred named peaks over
10,000 feet. Longs Peak, at 14,255 feet, is the highest in
the park and the most famous summit in the Front
Range north of Pikes Peak.

Roughly one-third of the park's area lies above tree
limit—a vast, gently rolling landscape of alpine tundra
with heroic, top-of-the-world vistas over a sea of
peaks. It is this fragile, weather-beaten realm of tiny
wildflowers and expansive panoramas that sets Rocky
Mountain apart from the rest of the national parks. In
no other will you find an alpine tundra zone as extensive and diverse as that found here. Nor will you find
tundra quite so accessible. Eleven miles of Trail Ridge
Road crosses the treeless zone, at roughly 12,000 feet.

As memorable as the tundra, and perhaps as
characteristic of Rocky, are the seductive, savanna-
like meadows of grass and ponderosa pine that stretch
among the eastern foothills. They're called parkland
meadows here, or "parks," as in Moraine Park, Estes
Park and others.

Between the parks and the tundra lie the forested
slopes of the mountains. From a distance, the forests

may appear as a uniform dark green band spreading across the mountains from bottom to tree limit. But certain tree species tend

Opposite: Longs Peak, 14,255 feet, rises between Mount Meeker and Mount Lady Washington.

to predominate in different areas, depending on elevation and exposure to sun, wind, and snow. In lower reaches of the park, lodgepole pine, aspen, ponderosa pine, and Douglas fir have found their respective niches. Shade-loving, cold tolerant species, such as Engelmann spruce, subalpine fir, and limber pine, predominate at higher elevations.

More than 150 small lakes glimmer in the glacial basins of Rocky Mountain's high country—many of them beneath cliffs soaring a thousand feet or more. Several important rivers, including the Colorado, have their headwaters within the park. And countless icy rivulets, cheerful brooks, and purling streams thread through the forests and wildflower meadows.

Living within this fabulous landscape are some of North America's most impressive hoofed animals: bighorn sheep, moose, elk, and mule deer. Gone are the small herds. Gone too are the wolves and grizzly bears that helped keep populations of hoofed animals in balance. But mountain lions still roam the park, and so do coyotes, pine martens, river otters, bobcats, badgers, weasels, and black bears.

Dozens of small rodents scurry through the underbrush, leap from tree limbs, burrow through the soil, or dart among the boulder fields and tundra meadows. Overhead fly birds of prey: hawks, owls, eagles, falcons. Even ravens have been known to take a mouse or two.

Besides these and other flesh-eating birds, the park comes alive each summer with an abundance of songbirds: meadowlarks, yellow warblers, goldfinches, warbling vireos, and western tanagers.

THE PARK'S GEOLOGIC HISTORY is relatively simple, but it does have its enigmatic moments. The rock structure here and the events that created the mountains are straightforward, but questions remain about exactly when certain important events occurred.

The park covers just a small portion of the Front Range, which extends from Wyoming to the vicinity of Colorado Springs. The core of the range is composed mainly of Precambrian gneiss, schist, and granite. This particular mass of gneiss and schist formed from volcanic and sedimentary layers about 1.7 billion years ago. The granite intruded the older rocks about 1.4 billion years ago.

For hundreds of millions of years, these rocks lay under or along the shore of ancient seas and accumulated a thick covering of sedimentary rock. It is not known how many times the sea advanced and retreated over what would become the Front Range, but we do know that the rocks rose about 300 million years ago as part of the Ancestral Rocky Mountains. That ancient mountain chain was completely leveled by erosion. The old Precambrian core sank beneath the sea again and started to accumulate more layers of sedimentary rock.

About 200 million years ago, a slow but incredibly powerful collision began between two of the Earth's tectonic plates off the west coast of North America. Pushed westward by the widening floor of the Atlantic ocean, the continental plate collided with and overrode the Pacific oceanic plate. Like an accordion, or a fender bender in slow motion, the margin of the continent gradually crumpled.

Roughly 65 million years ago, these titanic forces began the upheaval of today's Rocky Mountains. The initial upheaval lasted about 20 million years. During this time, the Front Range rose as a distinct block along fault lines running south to north. The range was pushed upward some 15,000 to 25,000 feet, but it never stood that high over the surrounding landscape because it eroded as it rose.

Later (some geologists say as recently as two million years ago), the entire intermountain region was heaved upward again. In Colorado, the land rose about 6,000 feet, and streams and rivers cut into the mountains with renewed vigor.

This erosion was augmented during the past 200,000 years by at least three major ice ages. Glaciers flowed down from the crest of the range, broadening and straightening the steep, stream-eroded valleys, piling up moraines, and gouging out spacious cirques in the high country. These long tongues of moving ice put the final touch on today's alpine scenery.

HUMANS ARRIVED in the area at the end of the last ice age. The earliest hunters may have simply passed through. Later, other prehistoric people built rock-walled structures that helped funnel elk, deer, and sheep along predictable routes and into the shooting range of waiting hunters.

Modern tribes, such as the Ute, moved into the area perhaps 1,500 years ago. For most of their history, the Ute lived among Colorado's mountains and high valleys, hunting elk, deer, and sheep and gathering edible plants. A couple of times a year, they ventured over the mountains to hunt buffalo (bison) on the plains. After they obtained the horse, the Ute spent far more time on the plains hunting buffalo, which became their primary food source. Other tribes had the same idea, and the Ute clashed with the Commanche and the Arapaho.

Eventually, all the tribes were forced from the mountains after gold and silver were discovered. Mountains in the park area yielded little in the way of mineral wealth, however, and it is in part due to this poverty that the park was established.

Settlement of the Estes Park and Grand Lake areas began during the 1860s, as small ranchers such as Joel Estes and his family moved into the valleys. Shortly, though, wealthy hunters, climbers, and other adventurous visitors offered a more dependable way for locals to make a living—as guides and innkeepers.

The richest hunter of them all, an Englishman named Windham Thomas Wyndham-Quin, the Fourth Earl of Dunraven, snapped up thousands of acres in shady land deals, built a high-brow hotel, and was widely despised. After his hotel burned down, he sold out.

Freelan Stanley, the wealthy inventor of the Stanley Steamer auto, bought much of Dunraven's land. In 1909, he opened a sumptuous hotel, the Stanley Hotel, which still overlooks Estes Park. The civic-minded Stanley, widely admired, backed the notion of setting aside a portion of the Front Range as a national park for everyone to enjoy.

No voice can take sole credit for suggesting the creation of Rocky Mountain National Park, but it's fair to say that Enos Mills was its most ardent and vocal partisan. Mills—cowboy, miner, climbing guide, and innkeeper—was a self-taught naturalist, lyrical writer of natural history, and a protégé of John Muir. In 1909, he suggested establishing a national park that would extend along the Front Range from Estes Park to the vicinity of Colorado Springs. Theodore Roosevelt backed the idea and asked Mills to travel the nation lobbying for the park's creation. Several years of promotion, debate, and compromise followed. The proposed boundaries shrank, and in 1915 Rocky Mountain National Park was formally dedicated.

Travelers' Information

SIX VISITOR centers located throughout the park stock brochures, books, and maps. Park staff is on hand to answer questions. Some centers offer interpretive films and exhibits. Newspapers published by the park and handed out at entrance stations list park services and seasonal schedules for ranger walks, talks, and other programs.

The visitor centers are located at Park Headquarters, on the US 36 approach to the park; on US 34 before the Fall River Entrance Station; Moraine Park Museum on the park's east side; at Lily Lake, south of Estes Park on Colo. 7; at Fall River Pass along Trail Ridge Road; and north of Grand Lake on the park's west side. All are open daily during the summer season. The Park Headquarters at Beaver Meadows and Kawuneeche Visitors Center at Grand Lake are open year round.

Entrance fees for Rocky Mountain are $15 per private vehicle, good for seven days. Bicyclists pay $5 for a weekly permit. An annual pass for Rocky Mountain costs $30. A National Parks Pass costs $50 and grants entry to all national parks for twelve months. A Golden Eagle Pass runs $65 and accesses all national parks and monuments for twelve months. Golden Age Lifetime Passports for U.S. residents 62 or older cost $10, and Golden Access Passports for the disabled are free; these also entitle the holder to reduced camping fees.

Correspondence and requests for information should be directed to: Superintendent, Rocky Mountain National Park, Estes Park, CO, 80517 (tel. 970-586-1206), *www.nps.gov/romo;* or the Estes Park Chamber Resort Association, 500 Big Thompson Ave., Estes Park, CO, 80517 (tel. 800-443-7837), *www.estesparkresort.com.*

Driving: Except where otherwise posted, the park's speed limit is 35 mph. Some roads, particularly the Old Fall River Road, are unsuitable for RVs. Gasoline is available in Estes Park and Grand Lake.

Because both Trail Ridge Road and Old Fall River Road climb to about 12,000 feet above sea level, people with respiratory or heart ailments are advised to consult their physicians before embarking.

Anyone unaccustomed to the elevation may come down with altitude sickness. Symptoms include nausea, dizziness, headache, rapid heartbeat, and shortness of breath. Drink lots of water, eat lightly, get plenty of rest, hike with caution, and avoid cigarettes and alcohol. Also, bear in mind that sunlight is far more intense at high elevations. Sunglasses, a hat, and sunscreen help prevent eye damage and sunburn.

Extremes in elevation also have a powerful effect on engine performance. Expect your vehicle to feel a bit sluggish, to start hard, and to use more gasoline on Trail Ridge and Old Fall River roads. It's easy to flood the engine, so back off on the gas pedal when starting. Overheating and vapor lock often strand motorists. Pull over to the side of the road—not on the vegetation —and wait for the engine to cool down.

Shuttle Bus Service: Because parking lots jam early on summer days at Bear Lake, Glacier Gorge, and other popular trailheads, the park operates a free shuttle bus service. The bus departs for Bear Lake every 30 minutes from a parking area across the road from Glacier Basin Campground. Shuttle service also extends from Moraine Park Museum to Glacier Basin, and from the museum to the Fern Lake Trailhead in Moraine Park. Bus stops are marked on the maps. An excellent service, the shuttle not only allows you to avoid the crowds but also to plan straight-line, one-way hikes rather than back-to-your-car loops.

A tour group bumps along the road to Bear Lake in the late 1920s.

Boating: Boating is permitted on lakes outside the park. Boating is not recommended in the park, but is permitted without motors on all park lakes except Bear Lake.

Fishing: Fishing requires a Colorado fishing license, available at local sporting goods stores. Park fishing regulations are designed to protect fish populations. For that reason, complicated rules that change from place to place apply to seasons, limits, sizes, and equipment. Pick up regulations at visitor centers.

Hiking: Driving is a good way to get an overall view of Rocky Mountain National Park, but a close-up look on foot is essential for a deeper understanding. There are many short trails just off the roads. Some have signs along the route or offer self-guiding booklets to help identify and explain interesting points.

Park naturalists and interpreters lead hikes and strolls that range in length from a half hour to four hours. These excellent interpretive hikes cost nothing and are conducted regularly from visitor centers and trailheads throughout the park. You'll find a list of nature walks and ranger talks in the park newspaper.

No permits are required for day-hiking, but some common-sense precautions are in order. Carry a trail map. Be prepared for sudden weather changes— especially above tree limit, where lightning is a very serious hazard. Bring food and water for any but a very short hike. Do not drink water from streams, lakes, or snowfields unless you treat it or boil it first.

Please stay on the trails. Alpine tundra plants grow as little as one-sixteenth of an inch per year. They are quickly and easily destroyed by foot traffic, and it can take centuries for denuded tundra to recover.

Horseback Riding: There are stables at Moraine Park and Sprague Lake on the Park's east side that offer guided trail rides. You can also rent horses from several liveries in the Estes Park and Grand Lake areas. More than 260 miles of park trails are open to horse travel. Regulations are available at the visitor centers.

Bicycling: Bicyclists are welcome in Rocky Mountain, but roads tend to be narrow with little or no shoulder. Bicycles are confined to established roads within the park, but there are hundreds of miles of trails in the national forests that adjoin the park. American Youth Hostels are located near Estes Park and Grand Lake.

Wheelchair Access: Many of the park's ranger walks and talks are wheelchair accessible, as are visitor centers, rest rooms, roadside view points, and many of the campsites in the developed campgrounds. At Sprague Lake, there are backcountry campsites accessible to wheelchairs.

Also, many of the park's most popular roadside trails can be navigated by wheelchair. These include the trails around Bear Lake and Sprague Lake, the trail to the Holzwarth Historic Site and the Tundra Communities Trail on Trail Ridge Road.

Wildlife: Rocky Mountain National Park offers one of the most rewarding wildlife viewing opportunities in the U.S. One need not work too hard to spot elk, moose, mule deer, bighorn sheep, coyotes, marmots, pikas, or squirrels. Also present, but rarely seen, are black bears, mountain lions, and bobcats.

Besides mammals, a tremendous variety of birds can be seen within the park. There are eagles, hawks, owls and, in the large lakes west of the park boundary, osprey. To these large birds of prey add ducks, hummingbirds, mountain bluebirds, ravens, jays, American dippers, and a host of songbirds.

Viewing wildlife should be done with care and sensitivity for the animals. Most will not tolerate the close approach of a human, and some will protect themselves when it happens. Among the park's larger animals, bull moose are especially dangerous. It's best to stay in or near your car if you come across an animal by the road.

Hikers take a breather on the slopes of Prospect Mountain to look back over early Estes Park and the Fall River Valley.

Feeding animals, large or small, is strictly forbidden. When animals become dependent on people for food, they congregate near roads and parking lots where they are more likely to be hit by cars and where they make easy targets for poachers. Some animals transmit diseases to humans. Others may bite.

Seasons: Snow can fall on any day of the year, including July 4. But winter does not generally close in on the Park as a whole until November. However, Old Fall River Road and most of Trail Ridge Road usually close for the season by mid-October. On the park's west side, plows keep Trail Ridge Road open to Timber Lake Trailhead. On the east side, Trail Ridge is maintained as far as Many Parks Curve. The road to Bear Lake is plowed all winter, as is the Moraine Park road as far as Cub Lake Trailhead. Roads generally open again in May, although Trail Ridge often remains partially closed until late May.

Spring (April and May) is a time of raucous, unsettled weather when rain, sleet, wet snow, and generally socked-in conditions prevail.

Summer begins in June for most of the park and extends through August, though it may not come to portions of the tundra until mid-July. Summer is when the park is at its scenic peak, when colorful patches of wildflowers smear the green meadows with blue, red, pink and yellow blossoms. This is also the season when the Park clogs with most of the three million visitors who come every year.

Autumn is a time of clear skies, thinning crowds, and aching beauty. The grasses of the parkland meadows turn golden brown. Shrubs take on a rusty hue, and the aspens change to bright yellow. Deer, elk, and bighorn sheep move out of the high country to the meadows for their annual mating rituals, and campers often awake to heavy frost or a dusting of snow.

Lodging: Aside from camping, there are no overnight accommodations within Rocky Mountain. However, there are several historic hotels and lodges along the park's borders. To name a few: the Stanley Hotel, the grande dame of Estes Park's hotels; the Baldpate Inn, a timber frame hostelry overlooking Estes Park; and Grand Lake Lodge, overlooking Grand Lake. There are dozens of other hotels, motels, and inns in Estes Park, Grand Lake, Meeker Park, and Allenspark. Summer is a busy season, so it's a good idea to book reservations well in advance. Call the Estes Park Chamber Resort Association, 800-443-7837; or the Grand Lake Chamber of Commerce, 800-531-1019.

Camping: There is a seven days limit between June and September, with the exception of Longs Peak Campground, where the limit is three nights.

Moraine Park, Longs Peak, and Timber Creek campgrounds are open year-round, though the drinking water is shut off in mid-September. Glacier Basin closes in early September, and Aspenglen Campground closes in late September.

A 1920s fisherman returns to camp at Bear Lake with tall tales and, apparently, no fish. Camping is no longer allowed at the lake.

Campgrounds provide basic services: tent pads, picnic tables, toilets, drinking water, and trash collection. There are no showers and no utility hookups for RVs. Fees are $18 per night. Campgrounds are jammed during summer. Those who begin to search for a site in late afternoon are often out of luck. Summer reservations are available for Glacier Basin and Moraine Park (tel. 800-365-2267).

Wood gathering is prohibited throughout the park, though firewood bundles are sold at the campgrounds. Fires must be built within fire grates, unless you have obtained a special permit.

Permits costing $15 per trip are required for all overnight outtings in the backcountry. Contact the Backcountry Office, Rocky Mountain National Park, Estes Park, CO 80517 (tel. 970-586-1242); *www.nps.gov/romo/visit/park/camping.html*; or stop at the Backcountry Office at Park Headquarters on the east side, or at the Kawuneeche Visitor Center on the west side.

Pets: While in the park, pets must be on a leash no longer than six feet, in a vehicle, or caged. They are not permitted on any trail.

Emergencies: Phone 911 or 970-586-1203.

Weather Information: For weather and road conditions, call 970-586-1333. For information about the park's west side, call the Kawuneeche Visitor Center, 970-627-3471.

National Forests: Additional camping, hiking, fishing and boating is available in the national forests adjoining the park. For information about Roosevelt National Forest (east side), call 970-498-2770. For information about Arapaho National Forest (west side), call 970-887-3331.

On the Road

Estes Park Townsite

THE VALLEY takes its name from Joel Estes, who homesteaded here from 1860 to 1866 with his wife and 14 children. They weren't the first to make a living from the valley. For thousands of years before the Estes ran cattle here, Ute, Arapaho, and other Native American groups hunted and perhaps lived, at least for part of the year, in the Estes Park area.

Other ranchers followed the Estes family, and within a decade a fledgling resort industry began adding to the settlement. Soon, hikers, hunters, scientists, and tourists were streaming into the Estes Park area. Its permanent status as a tourism center was assured in 1915 with the dedication of Rocky Mountain National Park.

Estes Park Area Historical Museum: Located at the corner of US 36 and Fourth Street, the museum houses exhibits photos, implements, and other memorabilia

Lake Estes: This lake was created after World War II as part of a major irrigation project that diverts water from the west slope of the Front Range to the eastern plains.

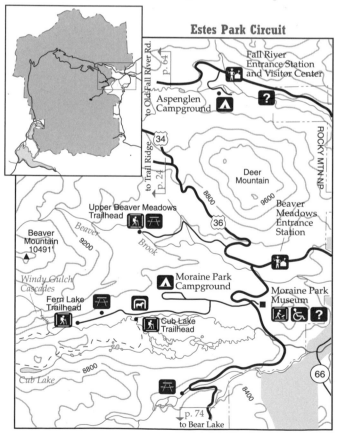

Estes Park Circuit

Devils Gulch Road: Beyond the rim of northern Estes Park, this road threads through Devils Gulch, a tortuous canyon of the North Fork Big Thompson River. A 1976 flash flood killed at least 140 people in Big Thompson Canyon. Several days of steady rain in late July culminated in a downpour of 8 to 12 inches in just four hours. Both the North Fork and main branch of the Big Thompson River rose to devastating heights, moving 20-foot boulders and huge blocks of concrete, smashing houses, motels, cabins bridges, and vehicles. Many of those killed drowned as they tried to outrun the flood waters by driving down the canyon. Some might have lived had they climbed to safety, as today's highway signs advise.

MacGregor Ranch: Open to the public, this working cattle ranch has a history stretching back to the early 1870s. Its 1,200 acres, with a magnificent view of Longs Peak, have been preserved as open space, and the 1896 MacGregor family home now serves as a museum.

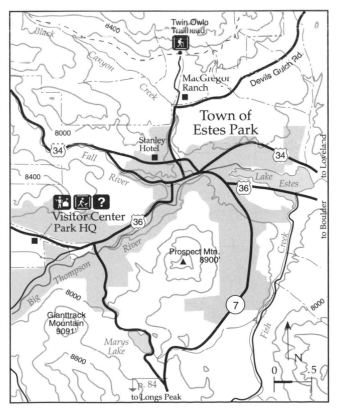

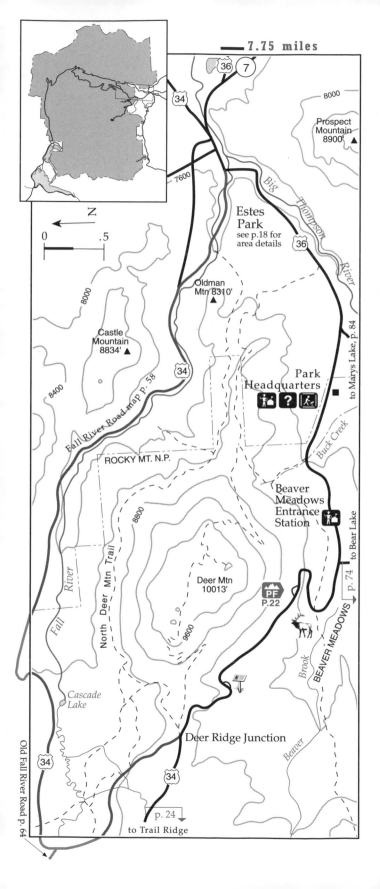

Estes Park: Broad, gently rolling, and ringed by knobby ridges, the Estes Park valley looks like a glacially-carved basin. Instead, it is a deep, stream-eroded canyon buried in mud and gravels that have washed out of the mountains.

High above town looms the park's scenic heart—a magnificent crest of gray rock, gouged by glaciers and split by the meandering watershed of the Continental Divide. The summits approach or exceed 13,000 feet and include Longs Peak, 14,255 feet high, on the far left.

Park Headquarters: This unobtrusive stone building overlooks a broad parkland meadow dotted with widely spaced ponderosa pines. Designed by Taliesen Associated Architects, it is listed is on the National Register of Historic Places. Inside, a short film presents an overview of the park. This is a good place to buy books, maps, posters, and videos.

Beaver Meadows Entrance Station: Here, Longs Peak and its companion mountains rise 6,000 to 7,000 feet above wide, grassy Beaver Meadows. Forests growing on the slopes of this abrupt rampart reflect the fact that climate varies with elevation. Broadly speaking, the higher you go, the harsher the conditions. This encourages a succession of forest species, each better adapted than the last to an increasingly severe climate that eventually bars the growth of all trees.

Climate variations group other plants and animals in similar fashion, loosely dividing the park into three zones, or ecosystems. Beaver Meadows lies in the Montane Ecosystem, where ponderosa pine and Douglas fir predominate and prairie flowers grow among the grass and dryland shrubs. Look for elk, mule deer, hawks, and owls.

Deer Ridge Junction: (Elev. 8937 feet) The Mummy Range swings into view on the right as westbound travelers approach this junction, which marks the official start of Trail Ridge Road. As it climbs to an elevation of 12,183 feet, the road winds through all of the park's major ecosystems, topping out far above tree line in the Alpine Tundra Ecosystem, where plants, animals, and climate resemble those of the Arctic Circle.

Across Upper Beaver Meadows

Stones Pk.
12,922 ft

Sprague Mtn.
12,713 ft

Knobtop Mtn.
12,331 feet

Notchtop Mtn.
12,129 ft

Flattop Mtn.
12,324 ft

Hallett Pk.
12,713 ft

Otis Pk.
12,486 ft

Taylor Pk.
13,153 ft

Taylor
Glacier

Thatchtop
12,668 ft

McHenrys Pk.
13,327 ft

Chiefs Head Pk.
13,579 ft

Longs Peak
14,255 ft

Mount
Lady Washington
13,281 ft

Mount Meeker
13,911 ft

South — Lateral — Moraine

22

Reading the Landscape

■ The Front Range ■ The peaks across the valley are part of the Front Range, which extends 180 miles from the Wyoming border to Colorado Springs. The rocks, mainly granite, gneiss, and schist, formed 1.45 to 1.75 billion years ago and remained buried for hundreds of millions of years. Then, starting roughly 65 million years ago, the core of what is now the Front Range slowly rose along two, nearly parallel fault zones. It was heaved upward bearing a cap of overlying sedimentary layers that eroded and washed out onto the plains.

■ Glaciation ■ During various ice ages, alpine glaciers gnawed away at the crest of the mountain core, carving out spacious amphitheaters and U-shaped troughs such as those seen today between Thatchtop and Taylor Peak, and along the ramparts of Notchtop, Knobtop, and Gabletop Mountains.

These smaller glaciers converged to form immense valley glaciers, which plowed down from the summits, piling up along their flanks heaps of rubble called lateral moraines. Two such moraines lie across Upper Beaver Meadows.

■ Longs Peak ■ The highest and best-known summit in the park, Longs Peak ranks 15th in elevation among Colorado's mountains. Rocks on its flat summit correspond with rocks buried deeply in the Denver Basin, rocks that lie 22,000 feet below the summit, indicating the vertical displacement of the mountains.

■ Ponderosa Parkland ■ The broad, rolling meadow at your feet typifies the grassy, open areas of the park's eastern foothills. Ponderosa pines—with a thick, reddish bark that smells of vanilla, butterscotch or pineapple—spread their branches over prairie grasses and wildflowers teeming with rodents. Mice, voles, shrews, and golden-mantled ground squirrels attract predators such as coyotes, badgers, hawks, and owls. Elk feed on the grasses and herbs; mule deer on bitterbrush and other shrubs. Bluebirds flit over the grasses. Nuthatches fidget on tree trunks. Hummingbirds work the wildflowers, and western tanagers flash their near-tropical colors of yellow and red. Silent, tassel-eared tree squirrels, called Abert's squirrels, live exclusively in the surrounding ponderosa pine forests and depend on the trees for food, nesting, and cover.

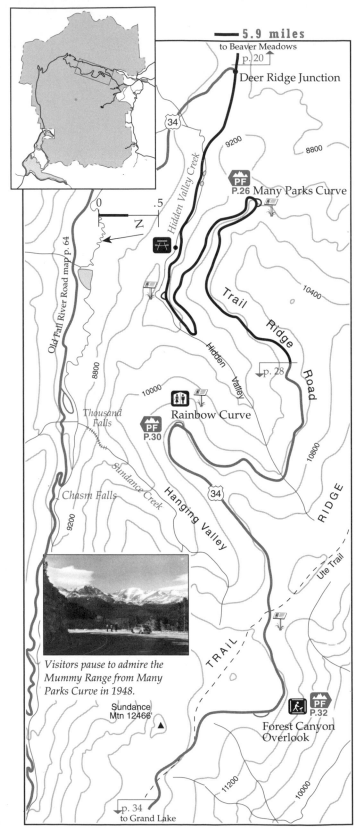

5.9 miles
to Beaver Meadows
p. 20

Deer Ridge Junction

34

9200

8800

P.26 Many Parks Curve

0 .5

N

Old Fall River Road map p. 64

Hidden Valley Creek

10400

Trail Ridge Road

p. 28

Hidden Valley

8800

10000

Rainbow Curve

P.30

Thousand Falls

Sundance Creek

Chasm Falls

9200

Hanging Valley

34

10800

RIDGE

Ute Trail

Visitors pause to admire the Mummy Range from Many Parks Curve in 1948.

TRAIL

Sundance Mtn 12466'

Forest Canyon Overlook

P.32

11200

10000

p. 34
to Grand Lake

Trail Ridge Road

Beaver-made Meadows: Surrounded by a mixed ever-green forest, this expansive wetlands meadow was until recently a network of large beaver ponds, dikes, and canals. For nearly 50 years the beavers maintained their dams, and the ponds collected a deep layer of silt and rich organic debris that washed down from Hidden Valley. Then in the late 1990s, the beavers abandoned the area. Their dams decayed, and the ponds drained, leaving behind fertile soil 20 feet deep.

Sedges, grasses, willows, and other vegetation quickly reclaimed the pond beds, creating this lush, wetlands meadow, where red-winged blackbirds natter among the blades of grass and tiger salamanders slither in the mud.

North of Hidden Valley Curve: For a couple of miles above the Hidden Valley hairpin turn, the road passes through a forest of lodgepole pine and aspen. Both species tend to pioneer areas opened up by forest fires, and that's what has happened here. A 1915 blaze cleared a section of the subalpine fir and Engelmann spruce forest that normally predominates here. The lodgepole and aspen quickly filled in.

Many Parks Curve: (Elev. 9620 feet) The boardwalk commands a sweeping vista of forested ridges, knobby mountains, and expansive meadows to the east. French trappers called the open, grassy areas *parques*, a name that stuck. Moraine Park lies to the right of Beaver Meadows, and you can see Horseshoe Park from the lower parking area. (See Peaks Finder, p. 26.)

From here, it's easy to imagine the glaciers—hundreds of feet deep and miles long—that covered the valleys 10,000 years ago and built up the forested, lateral moraines that run alongside the parks. Most of the parks were once glacial lake beds that filled with mud, silt and other debris.

Many Parks Curve lies high in the Montane Ecosystem, the second major ecosystem in the Park. The predominant tree species here are Douglas fir, limber pine, and lodgepole pine. Pine squirrels scramble through the trees, occasionally chased by big weasels called martens. Chipmunks scurry across the rocks. Also in this forest: porcupines, shrews, mice, great horned owls, ravens, and woodpeckers.

From Many Parks Curve

MUMMY RANGE

Mt. Chiquita
13,069 ft

Ypsilon Mtn.
13,514 ft

Fairchild Mtn.
13,502 ft

Hagues Pk.
13,560 ft

Mummy Mtn.
13,425 ft

Bighorn Mtn.
11,463 ft

Mount Dickinson
11,831 ft

Dark Mtn.
10,859 feet

MacGregor Mtn.
10,486 feet

Alluvial Fan from
the 1982 Flood

Horseshoe Park

Reading the Landscape

■ **Mummy Range** ■ These mountains extend north
for about ten miles, are part of the Front Range, and
share its same basic creation story. Local tradition,
rather than geologic distinction, sets them apart.
Early visitors imagined that the outline of these
peaks resembled a mummy. Good luck seeing
the resemblance.

■ **Ypsilon Mountain** ■ The peak was named for
fissures on its deeply glaciated east face. The fissures
hold snow late into the summer, clearly delineating
the letter Y, called Ypsilon in Greek.

■ **Bighorn Mountain** ■ This large, forested dome,
studded with smooth knobs of weathered granite,
takes its name from the frequent sightings of bighorn
sheep on its slopes. The bighorns descend throughout
the summer and cross into Horseshoe Park, where
they enjoy the salt licks that have formed around a
handful of ponds.

■ **Horseshoe Park** ■ The tail end of one of the park's
biggest valley glaciers once lay over Horseshoe Park.
It reached depths of 1,500 feet and extended from
Fall River Pass, at today's Alpine Visitor Center,
to the east end of Horseshoe Park. As it melted, the
glacier left a terminal moraine that dammed
the valley and created a lake. The fine-grained,
mud-and-sand soil that eventually filled in the lake
discourages trees from growing in Horseshoe Park,
and the flat terrain forces Fall River to meander
across the valley floor.

■ **Alluvial Fan** ■ The beige, triangular rock field lying
along the left flank of Bighorn Mountain is an alluvial
fan deposited by the Roaring River in a matter of
hours on July 15, 1982. An old earthen dam burst at
Lawn Lake (beneath Mummy Mountain, but out of
view), and a wall of water 25 to 30 feet high crashed
down the canyon, tumbling boulders and stones and
ripping out trees. The debris collected where you see
it, damming Fall River and creating a new lake (also
out of view). The flood continued down Fall River, its
violence checked though still extreme. Two campers
were killed at Aspenglen, where the banks of the river
are still strewn with boulders and tree trunks tossed
about by the flood.

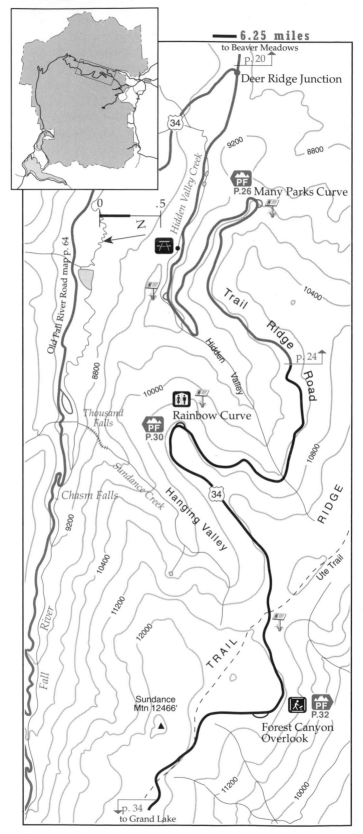

to Beaver Meadows
p. 20
Deer Ridge Junction

34

9200
8800

PF
P.26 Many Parks Curve

0 .5

N

Trail
Ridge
Road

10400

Hidden Valley Creek

Hidden Valley
p. 24

Old Fall River Road map p. 64

8800

10000
Rainbow Curve
PF
P.30

Thousand
Falls

Sundance Creek

Chasm Falls

9200

Hanging Valley

34

10800

RIDGE

Ute Trail

10400

11200

12000

TRAIL

Fall River

Sundance
Mtn 12466'

PF
P.32
Forest Canyon
Overlook

11200

10000

p. 34
to Grand Lake

Between Many Parks Curve and Rainbow Curve: Here the road passes through the Subalpine Ecosystem, where the dense, surrounding forest is made up of subalpine fir, Engelmann spruce, and limber pine. Spruce and fir tend to grow in the shallow ravines; limber pine on ridges exposed to wind.

More snow collects in subalpine forests than in any other mountain zone: 10 to 15 feet from the clouds; more from fierce winds blowing it off the tundra into subalpine valleys below. Snow lasts late into summer, acting as an obstacle for many animals, cutting short the growing season for understory plants, and providing a cool, moist environment.

Rainbow Curve: (Elev. 10,829 feet) Known for the spectacular rainbows often seen from here after thunderstorms, this point overlooks a vast section of the park's east side. The vista starts on the far right and takes in Longs Peak, Trail Ridge, part of the Great Plains, Estes Park, Horseshoe Park, and the Mummy Range. Pikas and marmots live in the boulder field. (See Peaks Finder, p. 30.)

Nature Note ■ Krummholz: Near Rainbow Curve the effects of an increasingly frigid, dry, and wind-hammering climate begin to show among the trees. Some, called "banner" trees, have been stripped by the wind of all their needles and branches except those growing to leeward. Others huddle behind large boulders, their branches twisted and deformed. Subalpine firs grow as dwarfs from here to tree line—some of them more than 300 years old yet just a few inches in diameter. This is the forest's last gasp, a transition zone between the subalpine and alpine tundra regions often called krummholtz ("crooked wood"). ■

Ute Trail: (Elev. 11,440 feet) Trail Ridge was named for the ancient footpath that leads across the tundra from this turnout. The trail crosses the Front Range, connecting the western valleys with the buffalo (bison) country of the Great Plains. Native groups, most recently Ute and Arapaho, traveled it for thousands of years.

Forest Canyon Overlook: (Elev. 11,716 feet) A short trail leads to one of the park's most spectacular vistas: the heavily glaciated rampart of peaks across Forest Canyon. (See Peaks Finder, p. 32.)

From Rainbow Curve

Mount Chapin
12,454 feet

Mount Chiquita
13,069 ft

Ypsilon Mtn.
13,514 ft

Fairchild Mtn.
13,502 ft

Hagues Pk.
13,560 ft

Mummy Mtn.
13,425 ft

Mount Dunraven
12,571 ft

Bighorn Mtn.
11,463 ft

Roaring River

Reading the Landscape

■ Mummy Range Glaciers ■ During the ice ages, glaciers churned through all the major eastern valleys of the Mummy Range and clawed at its highest peaks. The ice formed slowly near the crest of the range and flowed down into narrow chasms that looked much like the canyons that head east from Estes Park today. The glaciers wore away the twists and turns and broadened the chasms into spacious valleys.

■ How Glaciers Form ■ Glaciers form where winter snowfall exceeds summer melting. As snow depth increases, pressure compacts the crystals into hard, blue ice, which begins to flow like putty once it reaches thicknesses of 50 meters. Constantly replenished with new snow at its upper end, the glacier flows downward, picking up loose rocks, breaking off others, and scudding them along the underlying bedrock like a belt sander in extreme slow motion. It will continue to extend itself until its lower end reaches a climate warm enough to stop its advance. But even then, it will continue to flow, burrowing deeper and deeper into the trough it has carved for itself.

■ Tree limit ■ Tree limit hugs a line where mean summer temperatures average 50 degrees. But temperature, which varies with elevation, tells only part of the story. Deep snow can discourage tree growth even where temperatures exceed the 50-degree rule of thumb. Wind also has a profound effect, drying out trees when replacement water is trapped in frozen ground and blasting them with snow and ice particles. Trees also fail to grow where soils are too wet or too cold or too thin.

All this means that the elevation of tree limit varies broadly depending on location. In the park, it fluctuates between 11,000 and 12,000 feet. In Wyoming, it drops to 9,500 feet; in Montana, to 7,500 feet.

■ Pikas ■ These tiny hares (about the size of a fat hamster) dart about the talus field below the parking area. Pikas can not hibernate. So they must cut, dry, and stack enough grass and other plants to carry them through the ten-month winter. A big job for any rodent, the task is more burdensome for pikas, whose metabolic rates demand much more food than mammals of similar size living at lower elevation.

From Forest Canyon Overlook

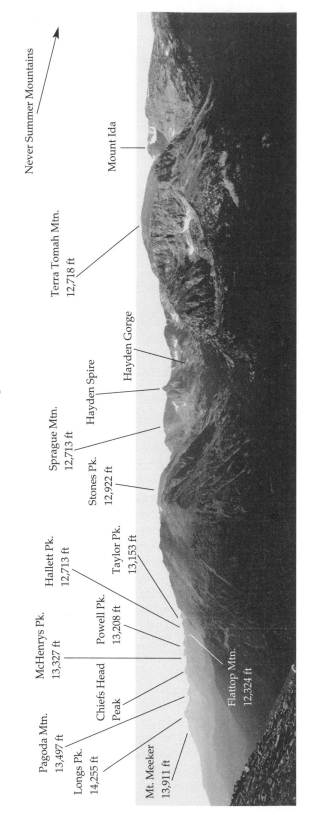

Never Summer Mountains

Mount Ida

Terra Tomah Mtn.
12,718 ft

Hayden Gorge

Hayden Spire

Sprague Mtn.
12,713 ft

Stones Pk.
12,922 ft

McHenrys Pk.
13,327 ft

Hallett Pk.
12,713 ft

Pagoda Mtn.
13,497 ft

Chiefs Head
Peak

Powell Pk.
13,208 ft

Taylor Pk.
13,153 ft

Longs Pk.
14,255 ft

Flattop Mtn.
12,324 ft

Mt. Meeker
13,911 ft

Reading the Landscape

■ **Forest Canyon** ■ Originally cut as a tortuous chasm by the Big Thompson River, Forest Canyon was gradually straightened and broadened into this capacious trough by one of the park's largest glaciers. It extended for 13 miles, exceeded depths of 2,000 feet, and was fed by a long series of smaller, alpine glaciers that flowed down from the peaks across the valley.

The canyon is one of the park's wildest areas. Trails neither lead into it nor rise from its floor to the glacial basins and peaks above. Mule deer, elk, black bears, mountain lions, beaver, squirrels, and rabbits all live in the canyon. Look for golden eagles soaring.

■ **Cirques** ■ The large, semi-circular hollows that appear along the crest of the range are called cirques. They are the birthplace and upper edge of the glaciers that bit deeply into these mountains. There is a cirque on the flank of Terra Tomah, one on either side of Hayden Spire, and several others at the top of Hayden Gorge.

As a glacier pulls away from the head end of its valley, a gap opens between ice and bedrock. Water and snow fill the gap and freeze to the bedrock. Then, as the glacier continues to move, it pulls away blocks of rock, actively eroding the upper end of its valley. The quarried blocks of rock continue to flow downward with the ice, gouging, rasping, polishing, and smoothing the underlying bedrock.

■ **Avalanche Chutes** ■ The long, diagonal stripes on the slopes of Stones Peak mark the tracks of recurring avalanches. These thundering slides of rock and snow can reach speeds exceeding 125 mph, ripping large trees out by their roots and clearing away all but the most pliable forms of vegetation. Alder, mountain maple, willow, mountain ash, and various berry bushes lie bent and crushed beneath the snow. When it melts, they bounce back, offering food for many animals.

■ **Naming the Landscape** ■ Many of the landmarks across Forest Canyon were named for those who explored, studied, or lived in the region. Longs Peak was named for an army officer; Powell Peak for John Wesley Powell, who made his name exploring the Colorado River. Stones and McHenrys Peaks were named for college professors; Hallett Peak, Sprague Mountain, Hayden Spire, and Hayden Gorge for local residents.

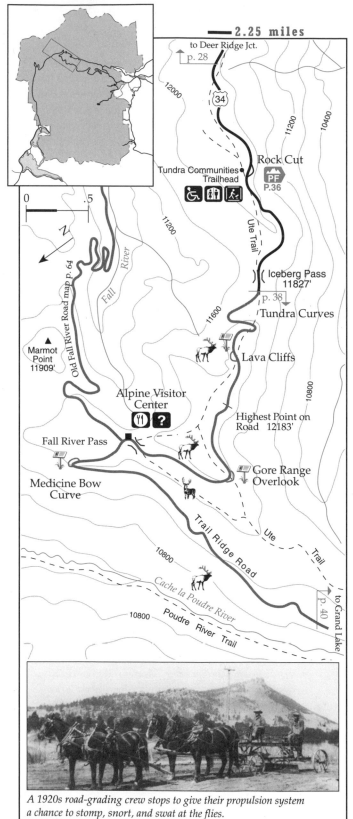

— **2.25 miles**

to Deer Ridge Jct.
p. 28

12000

34

11200

10400

Rock Cut
PF
P.36

Tundra Communities
Trailhead

11200

Ute Trail

Iceberg Pass
11827'
p. 38

Tundra Curves

11600

Lava Cliffs

10800

Marmot
Point
11909'

Alpine Visitor
Center

Highest Point on
Road   12'183'

Fall River Pass

Gore Range
Overlook

Medicine Bow
Curve

Old Fall River Road map p. 64

Fall River

Trail Ridge Road

Ute   Trail

to Grand Lake
p. 40

10800

Cache la Poudre River

10800

Poudre River Trail

0   .5

N

*A 1920s road-grading crew stops to give their propulsion system
a chance to stomp, snort, and swat at the flies.*

Trail Ridge: Above tree limit, the Alpine Tundra Ecosystem sprawls across the broad back of Trail Ridge. The tiny plants and handful of animals that live here cope with a ferocious environment.

First, it's cold. Temperatures average 20 degrees lower here than at Estes Park. The growing season lasts just six to eight weeks. Snow can fall at any time. Winds, which often exceed 100 mph and sometimes reach 200 mph, intensify the cold.

Second, it's dry. In spite of all the snow and dramatic summer thunderstorms, there is less effective precipitation here than anywhere else in the park. Evaporative rates are high. The sun shines with far greater intensity than at sea level. High winds accelerate evaporation and scour away snow. Thin, gravelly soils quickly drain moisture from the surface.

Rockcut: (Elev. 12,110 feet) Exhibits along the half-mile Tundra Communities Trail identify tundra plants and animals and describe how they have adapted to the cold, desert-like conditions. (See Peaks Finder, p. 36.)

Considering the challenges of this harsh climate, it should come as no surprise that the alpine tundra is a supremely fragile ecosystem, easily damaged and slow to recover. Plants often grow as little as one sixteenth of an inch per year, so it can take centuries to reclaim eroded areas. Please stay on the trails.

Nature Note ■ Survival of Alpine Plants: By hugging the ground, alpine plants avoid the worst of the weather, thus conserving moisture and warmth. Their small size reduces their needs for water and nutrients. Many flower and set fruit early because flowering does not require the heat of high summer while seed-ripening does. Others avoid the time-consuming process of setting seed by reproducing vegetatively.

Many tundra plants can grow in temperatures barely above freezing and carry on photosynthesis in colder conditions than their low-elevation counterparts. Many also contain anthocyanins, chemicals that warm plant tissue by converting light into heat. Some, like moss campion, conserve moisture by growing as compact cushion plants. Or, like spring beauties, some sink deep taproots. Leaves may have a waxy, leathery surface to slow evaporation. ■

From Rock Cut Overlook

Sprague Mtn.
12,713 ft

Hayden Spire

Terra Tomah Mtn.
12,718 ft

Mount Julian
12,928 ft

Cracktop

Mount Ida

Gorge Lakes

NEVER SUMMER MOUNTAINS

Reading the Landscape

■ **Gorge Lakes** ■ The wide, glaciated gorge to the right of Terra Tomah contains a string of small alpine lakes, known collectively as the Gorge Lakes. Two are plainly visible from this point: Arrowhead Lake, beneath Mount Ida; and Rock Lake, which lies at the foot of Terra Tomah. Each fills a deep depression gouged out of the bedrock by a glacier.

■ **Hanging Valley** ■ The 800-foot cliff beneath Arrowhead Lake marks the abrupt edge of a hanging valley. Hanging valleys form where a tributary glacier joins a much larger glacier. The tributary glacier, which in this case flowed down to Arrowhead Lake from the Continental Divide, does not cut as deeply as the main glacier. When the glaciers melt, the tributary valley is left hanging above the main valley.

■ **Arêtes** ■ These are the knife-edged ridges formed when two glaciers gnaw away on opposite sides of a mountain and nearly succeed in carrying off of the intervening rock. There's one between Mount Julian and Cracktop.

■ **Terra Tomah** ■ Terra Tomah has a convoluted naming history. The words "terra tomah" (unknown meaning) are supposedly Cohuila Indian chants overheard by a couple of Pamona College boys in 1892. Written into a glee club song, the words were carried into these mountains by a young climber who used them whenever the scenery delighted him.

■ **Alpine Animals** ■ Many animals pass through the alpine tundra, but few live here throughout the year. During warmer months, elk, mule deer, bighorn sheep, mountain lions, coyotes, and bobcats visit the tundra to graze or to hunt. But come winter, they head for lower climes.

Animals that remain depend on various strategies to survive. Marmots, golden-mantled ground squirrels, and pocket gophers hibernate. Pikas and bushy-tailed woodrats cache food. Active at night, deer mice huddle in groups during winter days, entering a torpor during which their body temperatures drop to conserve energy. Long-tailed weasels (whose skinny bodies demand a high metabolic rate) hunt all winter, caching dozens of rodent bodies in their grass-lined burrows to be eaten at leisure.

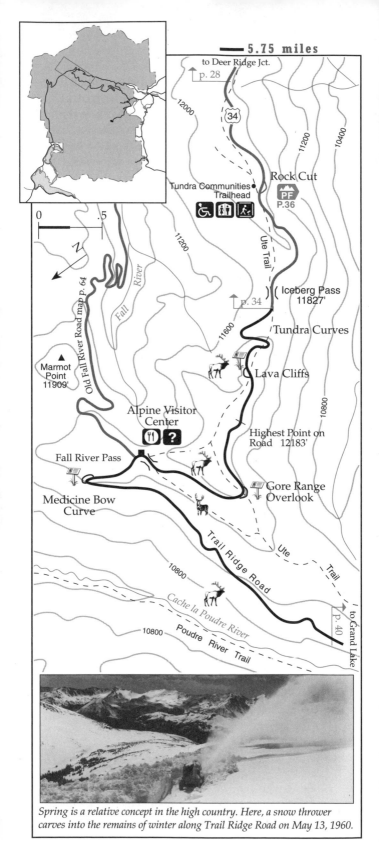

to Deer Ridge Jct.
p. 28

5.75 miles

US 34

12000

11200

10400

Rock Cut
P.36

Tundra Communities
Trailhead

11200

Ute Trail

p. 34

Iceberg Pass
11827'

Tundra Curves

11600

Fall River

Lava Cliffs

Marmot
Point
11909'

Old Fall River Road map p. 64

Alpine Visitor
Center

Highest Point on
Road 12183'

10800

Fall River Pass

Gore Range
Overlook

Medicine Bow
Curve

Trail Ridge Road

Ute   Trail

to Grand Lake
p. 40

10800

Cache la Poudre River

10800

Poudre River Trail

*Spring is a relative concept in the high country. Here, a snow thrower
carves into the remains of winter along Trail Ridge Road on May 13, 1960.*

Tundra Curves: Much of the tundra is covered with a thick mat of grass-like plants called sedges, which grow in tight bunches. One type, superturf sedge, lives only in areas blown free of snow and can actually grow in temperatures below freezing. To survive, it needs at least four inches of humus, a rich soil that accumulates on the tundra at a rate of an inch every thousand years. Turf sedges and grasses feed elk, deer, bighorn sheep, pikas, marmots, voles, and ground squirrels.

Lava Cliffs: (Elev. 12,085 feet) These walls of tuff (welded volcanic ash) formed about 28 million years ago as a volcano erupted in the Never Summer Range. Molten ash flowed east across the Specimen Mountain area roughly to this point, where it stopped and hardened. During the ice ages, snow blew across the broad back of Trail Ridge and collected below the cliffs, eventually helping to form an immense glacier. About 400 feet below the cliffs, a lush alpine meadow often draws a dozen or more elk.

Between Lava Cliffs and the Gore Range overlook, the road reaches its highest point: 12,183 feet.

Nature Note ▪ Dramatic Weather: Though perfectly clear in the morning, the sky can fill with turbulent afternoon thunderstorms that shake the ground with percussive thunderclaps and flog the tundra with rain, lightning bolts, and hail. These are often convective storms, which form after the sun has warmed the ground, causing moist air to rise into cooler altitudes. There, moisture condenses into boiling cumulous clouds that sweep in from the west and explode over Trail Ridge. ▪

Alpine Visitor Center: (Elev. 11,796 feet) The log frame fitted to the building's roof testifies to the severity of the winter weather. Exhibits offer a primer on the climate, plants, and animals of the alpine tundra. At the back of the building, a viewing platform overlooks a broad, glacially-carved basin covered with thick mats of sedges, grass, wildflowers, low shrubs, islands of dwarf subalpine fir, and, often, a small herd of elk.

Medicine Bow Curve: (Elev. 11,640 feet) From here, a sea of broad-shouldered peaks extends far to the northeast and includes parts of the Medicine Bow Mountains. On clear days, you can see Wyoming's Snowy Range, 44 miles away to the north.

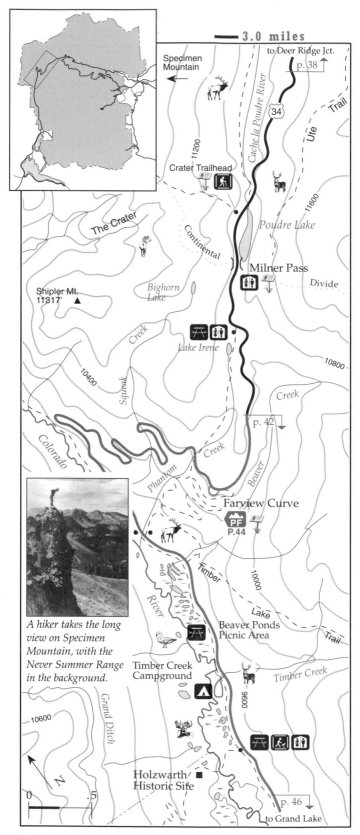

─── **3.0 miles**

to Deer Ridge Jct.

p. 38

Specimen Mountain

34

Cache la Poudre River

Ute Trail

11200

Crater Trailhead

Poudre Lake

The Crater

Continental

11600

Milner Pass

Shipler Mt. 11317'

Bighorn Lake

Divide

Squeak Creek

Lake Irene

10800

10400

Creek

Colorado

p. 42

Phantom Creek

Beaver

Farview Curve

PF P.44

A hiker takes the long view on Specimen Mountain, with the Never Summer Range in the background.

River

Timber

10000

Lake

Trail

Beaver Ponds Picnic Area

Timber Creek

Timber Creek Campground

0600

10600

Grand Ditch

Holzwarth ■ Historic Site

N

0   .5

p. 46

to Grand Lake

Specimen Mountain: The bulky, round-sided mountain across the valley to the west is composed of layer upon layer of volcanic rocks. The rocks piled up 28 million years ago, when vents in the immediate area spewed ash and lava and precipitated vast mudflows.

Cache la Poudre Valley: This impressive trough cradles the headwaters of the Cache la Poudre River, which flows northeast. The valley—deep, straight, steep-sided, and spacious—was carved by a glacier. Trees do not grow on its flat floor because the soil is too dense and too wet.

Nature Note ■ Wind-hammered Trees: Look for mule deer and elk feeding in the clearings between thickets of dwarf subalpine fir trees and stands of wind-hammered Engelmann spruce. Wind profoundly affects the way dwarf subalpine fir form into thickets. It forces seedlings to establish themselves in the shelter of rocks, dead trees, or shallow depressions. Then the tree grows to leeward, filling in the zone of protection it has created for itself and setting roots where its branches touch the ground. Eventually, it can spread over a large area and, perhaps joined by other seedlings, form what's called a tree island. In effect, the trees grow horizontally and, over time, actually migrate across the landscape. ■

Crater Trailhead: This steep, one-mile trail climbs through a subalpine forest on Specimen Mountain to the rim of a broad, semi-circular valley where bighorn sheep often graze. The trail remains closed until mid-July so the sheep can lamb in peace.

Poudre Lake: This is the source of the Cache la Poudre River, which meanders across the verdant subalpine meadow to the northeast. Dammed by a moraine, the lake may eventually fill in with silt and decomposed plant matter to become a meadow.

At the lake's south end, the road crosses Milner Pass and the Continental Divide at 10,758 feet. Rain falling in the lake runs to the Atlantic Ocean. Water dripping off the nearby outhouse roof flows toward the Pacific. More than a watershed, the divide also splits the park's climate. The west side gets nearly twice the moisture and has colder winters and much less wind than the east side.

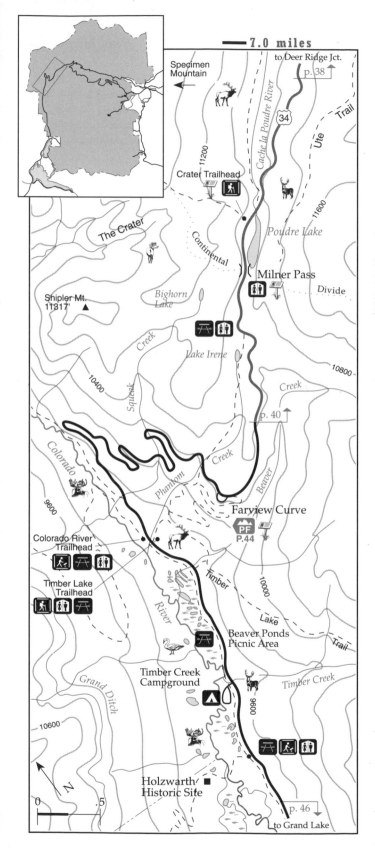

Specimen
Mountain

to Deer Ridge Jct.
p. 38

34

Ute
Trail

Cache la Poudre River

11200

Crater Trailhead

11600

Poudre Lake

The Crater

Continental

Milner Pass

Divide

Shipler Mt.
11317'

Bighorn
Lake

Squeak Creek

Lake Irene

10800

10400

Creek

p. 40

Colorado

9600

Phantom Creek

Beaver Creek

Farview Curve

PF
P.44

Colorado River
Trailhead

Timber Lake Trailhead

Timber

Lake

River

10000

Beaver Ponds
Picnic Area

Timber Creek
Trail

Timber Creek
Campground

Grand Ditch

9800

10600

Holzwarth
Historic Site

N

0   .5

p. 46

to Grand Lake

7.0 miles

42

Farview Curve (Elev. 10,120 feet) Perched over a thousand feet above the Kawuneeche Valley, this stop presents a grandstand view of the Never Summer Mountains and the meandering course of the infant Colorado River. (See Peaks Finder, p. 44.) Beside the turnout stand lodgepole pine, Engelmann spruce, and aspen.

Colorado River Trailhead The trail follows the narrow Colorado River upstream through a forest of lodgepole pine and aspen. It passes beaver ponds and leads 3.6 miles to the site of Lulu City, where faint traces remain of an 1880s mining town.

Kawuneeche Valley: Forests of mature lodgepole pine grow on both sides of this broad, glacial valley. The lodgepoles replace a climax forest of Engelmann spruce and subalpine fir that was destroyed in 1871 by a wide-ranging forest fire. Lodgepole, rather than spruce and fir, filled in the open areas because lodgepole grows better in open, sunny conditions.

However, spruce and fir hold the long-run advantage because they tolerate shade better than lodgepole. As a result, the young spruce and fir trees now growing in the shadow of the lodgepole canopy are expected to become the predominant tree species in the decades ahead.

Beaver Ponds Picnic Area: The picnic area lies close to an extensive wetland area dotted with several beaver ponds. The beaver has adapted not only to life in the water, but also to the physical demands of felling and dragging trees. Its massive skull allows it to slice into large trees, and its sharp teeth are broad and stout, like wood chisels.

Holzwarth Historic Site: Nestled into the forest fringe across the valley floor stands the preserved buildings of a 1920s-era dude ranch. John Holzwarth and family moved there after Prohibition shut down their Denver saloon. They started as ranchers, but found they could make more money charging guests $11 a week for room, board, and a horse. It's a half-mile walk to the cluster of buildings, some of which still contain their original furnishings. Now part of the park, the ranch is open for tours; ask at a visitor center for hours.

From Farview Curve

Lulu Mtn.
12,228 ft

Thunder Pass

Lead Mtn.
12,537 ft

Mount Cirrus
12,797 ft

Howard Mtn.
12,810 ft

Mount Cumulus
12,725 ft

Red Mtn.
11,605 ft

Mount Nimbus
12,706 ft

Mount Stratus

Green Knoll

Bowen Mtn.

KAWUNEECHE VALLEY

Grand Ditch

Reading the Landscape

■ **Never Summer Mountains** ■ Perhaps the most jagged set of mountains in the park, the Never Summer Mountains extend for about 15 miles and tower some 3,500 feet above the floor of the Kawuneeche Valley.

The Never Summers have a complex geology. Like most of the park's mountains, the southern end of the range is made up of Precambrian gneiss, schist, and granite. The northern three quarters are a mass of igneous rocks that flowed into this section of the Earth's upper crust 60 to 70 million years ago. At the same time, the rocks were shoved from east to west along an overthrust fault. Later, they were heaved upward, draped with ash and lava from nearby volcanoes, and then vandalized benevolently by glaciers.

■ **Kawuneeche Valley** ■ Pronounced "*kah-wuh-NEE-chee*," the Arapaho word means coyote. It's an appropriate name for this spacious valley where coyotes stalk the grassy meadows for deer mice, voles, shrews, and ground squirrels. The largest glacier in the park plowed out the Kawuneeche. It formed at least three times in the past 200,000 years, and its ice extended far south through Shadow Mountain Lake and north beyond La Poudre Pass. Thousands of feet thick, it covered all but the highest peaks and gathered in tributary glaciers from the Never Summers and the peaks south of Milner Pass.

■ **Colorado River** ■ The unlikely squiggle meandering across the open valley floor is the infant Colorado River, the same river that brawls through the Grand Canyon. Rising from snowfields along the Continental Divide west of Specimen Mountain, the Colorado used to flow into the Pacific Ocean at the Sea of Cortez. But the many irrigation projects that tap the river throughout its course now divert so much water that in many years it peters out some 20 miles short of the sea.

■ **Grand Ditch** ■ The slanting scar that runs across the flank of the Never Summers is an irrigation canal, the first of many diversions along the Colorado River. It collects meltwater from the peaks and pours roughly 20,000 acre feet of water each year over the Continental Divide into Long Draw Reservoir. From there it flows to farms, ranches, and towns on the eastern plains.

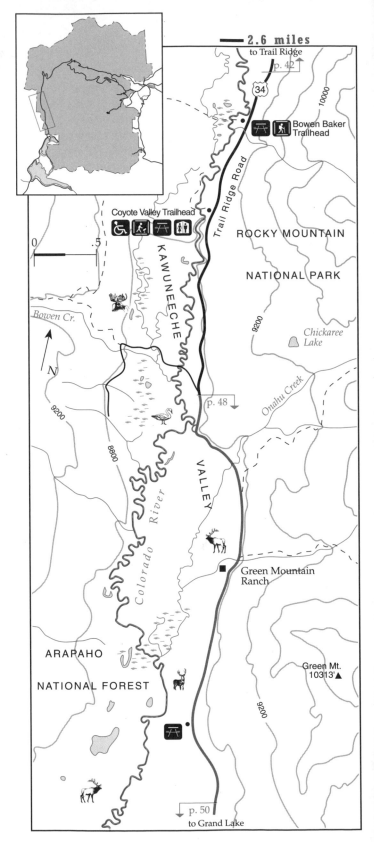

2.6 miles
to Trail Ridge
p. 42

34

Bowen Baker
Trailhead

Trail Ridge Road

Coyote Valley Trailhead

ROCKY MOUNTAIN

NATIONAL PARK

KAWUNEECHE

10000

9200

*Chickaree
Lake*

Bowen Cr.

N

9200

8800

p. 48

Onahu Creek

VALLEY

Colorado River

Green Mountain
Ranch

ARAPAHO

NATIONAL FOREST

Green Mt.
10313'▲

9200

p. 50
to Grand Lake

0   .5

Valley Floor: Lovely from a distance, fascinating close up, the open, meadow floor of the Kawuneeche Valley stretches for miles and supports a lush growth of waist-high prairie grasses, wildflowers, and shrubs. It's easy to find trails made by deer, elk, and moose crossing from the forests to the river. The meadow also provides homes for ground squirrels, chipmunks, mice, voles, and other rodents, who are in turn hunted by coyotes, badgers, hawks, and owls. Nighthawks dip over the grass snatching up insects.

Rich meadows in the proximity of forest cover make this valley ideal habitat for elk. These large animals are conspicuous during their autumn rut. Bulls challenge one another and lure cows with a distinctive bugling sound, a soaring squeal—starting on low notes and gaining range—followed by a series of abrupt, hoarse grunts that can be heard miles away. The bulls herd the cows, raid one another's harems, and occasionally spar each other with clattering antlers. Despite all the posturing, many biologists believe that it is the cow who gets to choose.

Mule deer are also common in the meadows and forests of the Kawuneeche Valley. They browse mostly on evergreen twigs, saplings, and shrubs. They owe their name to their large ears, a useful adaptation in open areas where faint sounds carry over long distances. 'Mulies' tend to congregate in herds, the better to detect predators.

Coyote Valley Trail: This broad, firm, and relatively flat trail crosses the Colorado River and follows it upstream for half a mile. Suitable for strollers or wheelchairs, the trail offers excellent exhibits on streamside ecology, wildlife, glaciation, and other fascinating topics. A branch of the trail leads to a pleasant picnic area along the fringe of the forest.

The word *Kawuneeche* is an Arapaho word for *coyote*. These wild dogs, common in the valley, are renowned for their cunning, and rightly so. For example, they often follow badgers. When the badger starts digging into a ground squirrel burrow, the coyote finds the emergency exit and jumps any squirrel that makes a run for it. Not in the least bit finicky, they eat just about anything: rodents, rabbits, roadkill, birds, insects, snakes, and plan. Listen in the evenings for their plaintive cries.

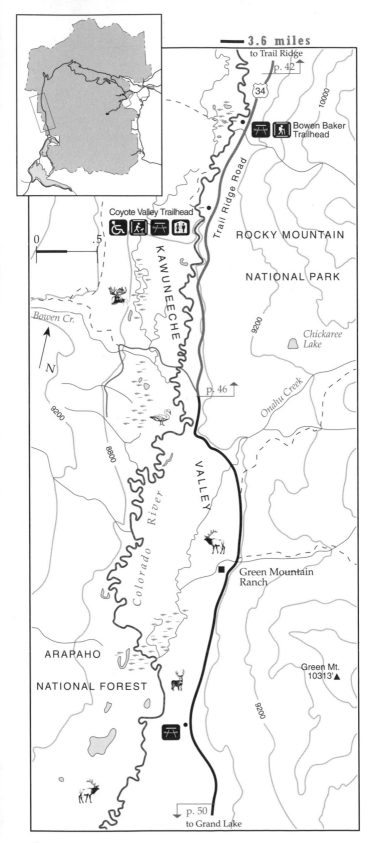

3.6 miles
to Trail Ridge
p. 42

34

Bowen Baker
Trailhead

Coyote Valley Trailhead

ROCKY MOUNTAIN

KAWUNEECHE

NATIONAL PARK

10000

9200

*Chickaree
Lake*

0   .5

Bowen Cr.

N

9200

8800

p. 46

Onahu Creek

Colorado River

VALLEY

Trail Ridge Road

■ Green Mountain
Ranch

ARAPAHO

NATIONAL FOREST

Green Mt.
10313' ▲

9200

p. 50
to Grand Lake

Onahu Creek: North of this creek crossing, look for moose among the wetlands of the Colorado. Eliminated from the park by settlers' rifles, moose are making a comeback. In 1977, 12 moose were reintroduced to North Park, west of the Never Summer Mountains. The moose thrived and spread into the Kawuneeche, where they might be seen browsing along the river.

Bull moose have the most massive antlers of all animals. They can span six feet and exceed weights of 70 pounds. Excellent swimmers, moose have been known to dive 15 feet for salt-rich aquatic plants. Their long legs are adapted for high-stepping through the snow; their broad hooves, for providing support in marshy areas. Moose browse on twigs, shrubs, and bark in winter; leaves, water plants, forbs, and grasses in summer.

Streamside: The moist river banks and wetland areas of the Kawuneeche support a diverse array of plants, which in turn support many animals. Thickets of shrubs often choke approaches to the stream. Forbs, grasses, sedges, rushes, climbing vines, and weeds are common at water's edge, and many types of aquatic plants grow in the ponds. This abundance of vegetation provides food, cover, and sites for nests, burrows, and dens. A variety of ducks nest in the Kawuneeche wetlands, as well as warblers, goldfinches, flycatchers, and belted kingfishers.

Many small mammals, including mice, voles, and ground squirrels, scurry through the underbrush. One of the most intriguing is the water shrew. Just three inches long (including tail), it dives for aquatic insects and kills frogs and fish larger than itself.

Nature Note ■ River Otters: Recently reintroduced to the park's west side, these sleek, playful animals live along the Colorado, slipping into the current for fish and rummaging along the banks for frogs, mammals, and birds. Dense fur, webbed feet, short legs, large lungs, and a long tail that acts as a rudder all adapt the otter to life in the water. Poor diggers, they den in abandoned beaver lodges and burrows of other animals. Intelligent and tenacious, otters have been known to pull apart beaver dams and then wade into the diminished pond to gorge on trapped fish and frogs. They also launch submerged assaults on waterbirds and kill muskrats in their burrows. ■

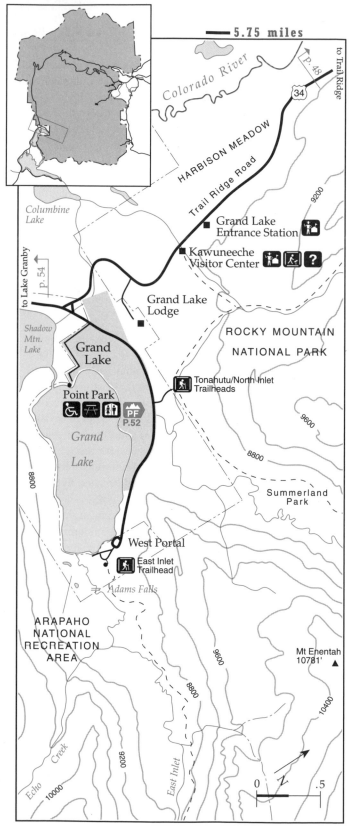

5.75 miles

to Trail Ridge

Colorado River

P. 48

34

HARBISON MEADOW

Trail Ridge Road

Columbine Lake

Grand Lake Entrance Station

Kawuneeche Visitor Center

to Lake Granby

P. 54

Grand Lake Lodge

ROCKY MOUNTAIN

NATIONAL PARK

Shadow Mtn. Lake

Grand Lake

Point Park

P.52

Tonahutu/North Inlet Trailheads

Grand Lake

8800

8800

9600

Summerland Park

West Portal

East Inlet Trailhead

Adams Falls

ARAPAHO NATIONAL RECREATION AREA

Mt Enentah 10781'

9600

8800

9200

10400

Echo Creek

East Inlet

10000

0   .5

Trail Ridge/Grand Lake

Kawuneeche Visitor Center: Exhibits in this small, informative museum focus on the plants, animals, and history of the park's west side. Short films acquaint visitors with the park as a whole, and rangers are on hand to answer questions and to issue backcountry camping permits. A self-guiding trail runs alongside the building and identifies common wildflowers, shrubs, and trees.

Grand Lake Lodge: About a mile off the road, the verandah of this historic 1920s lodge commands a terrific vista of Grand Lake and the surrounding mountain peaks.

Grand Lake: This beautiful alpine lake, surrounded by dense lodgepole forests and high, glaciated peaks, began attracting tourists as early as 1868. The town kicked into high and sometimes murderous gear during the 1880s mining boom along the North Fork Colorado River. A political rivalry with Hot Sulphur Springs led to a July 4, 1883, shoot-out west of town. Four died in the battle; two more in the bitter aftermath. They included three county commissioners, a county clerk, sheriff, and deputy.

Those familiar with large mountain lakes in the Rockies may be surprised that Grand Lake once rated as Colorado's largest natural lake. It's as big as ever (less than a mile wide and 1.5 miles long), but lost its natural designation when it became a reservoir for the east slope.

Nature Note ■ Chickarees and Fairydiddles: Abundant in conifer forests, red squirrels go by a variety of names including pine squirrel, chickaree, even fairydiddle. Whatever you call them, it's hard to miss these noisy, tail-flicking rodents. Bold, aggressive, territorial in the extreme, red squirrels dash out on tree limbs to scold passersby. They scramble through the forest at high speed, sometimes leaping and falling tens of yards between trees, suffering no apparent harm. They eat mostly pine seeds and pine nuts, but they also raid birds' nests for eggs and nestlings, devour insects and mice, and hang various fungi out to dry before caching them. Pine martens (large weasels) are one of the few predators that can chase red squirrels through the trees and kill them. ■

From Grand Lake

Summerland Park

Continental Divide

Mount Enentah
10,781 ft

Ptarmigan Mtn.
12,324 ft

Mount Cairns

Mount Craig
12,007 ft

Mount Wescott
10,421 ft

Reading the Landscape

■ **Grand Lake** ■ (Elev. 8367 feet) This lake formed after the glaciers of the last ice age retreated. A glacier flowing between Mount Bryant and Mount Enentah scooped out the deep depression now occupied by the lake and left the terminal moraine that now dams its west end.

■ **Glacial Troughs** ■ The two broad, U-shaped valleys that lead down to the lake mark the tracks of ice age glaciers. The valley to the right frames Mount Craig. Large glaciers flowed alongside the mountain's north and south flanks, joined at the base of the prominent cliffs seen from here, and then oozed into the Grand Lake basin.

The left-hand valley was carved by a single, large glacier which formed along the Continental Divide and flowed down the north side of Mount Enentah.

■ **West Portal** ■ This is the mouth of the 13.1-mile Alva B. Adams Tunnel, which was bored through the core of the Front Range and began supplying water in 1947 to east-slope farms, ranches, and towns. As the linchpin of the Colorado Big Thompson Water Diversion Project, the tunnel sucks as much as 550 cubic feet of water per second from Grand Lake, Shadow Mountain Lake, and Lake Granby. The water exits the tunnel southwest of Estes Park and collects in Lake Estes before flowing down the Big Thompson River Canyon toward the plains. Along the way several hydropower plants run the water through turbines to generate electricity.

During the 1930s, some of the park's rangers patrolled the roads on motorcycles.

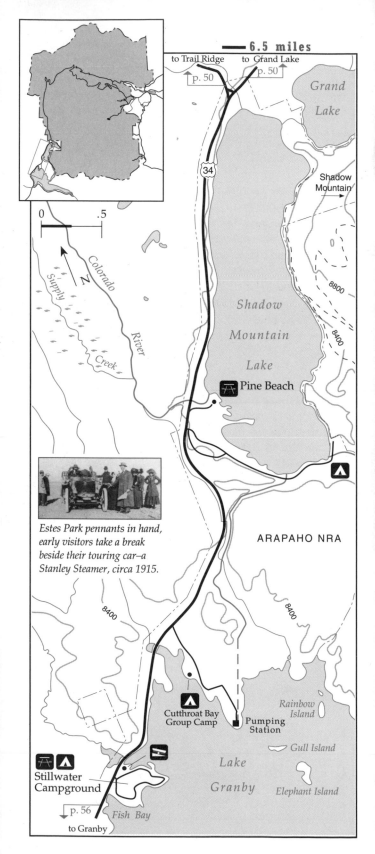

6.5 miles

to Trail Ridge   to Grand Lake
p. 50   p. 50

Grand

Lake

34

Shadow
Mountain →

0   .5

Supply   *Colorado*

Creek   *River*

N

Shadow

Mountain

Lake

🏕 Pine Beach

8800

8400

▲

*Estes Park pennants in hand,
early visitors take a break
beside their touring car–a
Stanley Steamer, circa 1915.*

ARAPAHO NRA

8400   8400

*Rainbow
Island*

▲
Cutthroat Bay
Group Camp   ■ Pumping
Station

Gull Island

🏕 ▲
Stillwater
Campground

*Lake
Granby*

Elephant Island

↓ p. 56
Fish Bay
to Granby

54

Shadow Mountain Lake: Roughly three miles long and a mile across, Shadow Mountain Lake is an artificial lake created in the 1940s as part of the Colorado–Big Thompson Water Diversion Project. Park Service officials fought the project as early as the 1920s on the grounds that the park already contained 18 irrigation projects and that the planned diversion tunnel through the mountains would further mar the wilderness qualities of the park. However, the political leverage of east-slope farmers, combined with the job-hungry atmosphere of the Great Depression, prompted President Roosevelt to approve the project in 1937.

Shadow Mountain Lake is part of the Arapaho National Recreation Area, a 33,000-acre preserve that also embraces Lake Granby and other elements of the diversion project.

Shadow Mountain: The deeply forested dome of granite, gneiss, and schist across the lake was named for the shadow it casts on the water. The trail on its southwest flank climbs 4.8 miles to a 1932 fire lookout listed on the National Register of Historic Places. The tower offers a splendid view over the trees to Grand Lake, Shadow Mountain Lake, Lake Granby, the East Inlet Valley, Mount Craig, Ptarmigan Mountain, and Andrews Peak.

Pine Beach: Lodgepole pines surround this lovely picnic area on the shore of Shadow Mountain Lake. Osprey nest on nearby islands and soar over the reservoir, hunting for trout, kokanee salmon, and other fish. A wetland area between the shore and the islands attracts Canada geese, mergansers, mallards, wood ducks, grebes, and loons. Beavers often swim through the channels between the shore and the islands early or late in the day. River otters also show up from time to time, swimming or bounding in their serpentine manner along the shore.

Stillwater Campground: The large block building across the lake from this campground is a pumping station for the Colorado–Big Thompson Water Diversion Project. The station lifts water from Lake Granby and sends it to Shadow Mountain Lake by way of a canal.

The high, jagged summits to the southeast are the Indian Peaks. The crest marks the Continental Divide and lies in the popular Indian Peaks Wilderness Area.

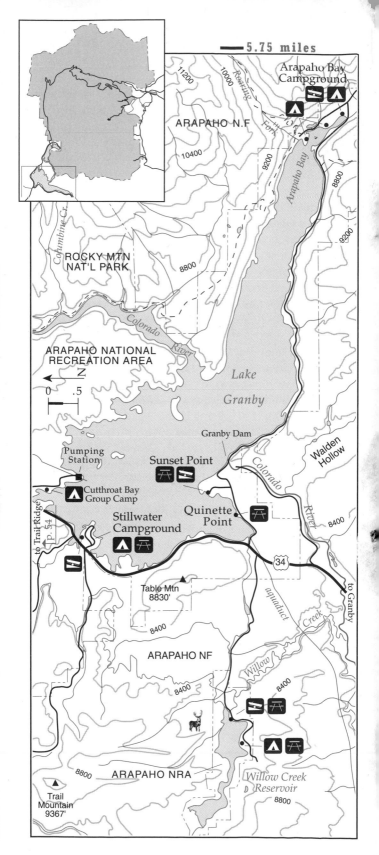

5.75 miles

Arapaho Bay Campground

11200

10000

Roaring Fork

ARAPAHO N.F

10400

9200

Arapaho Bay

8800

9200

Columbine Cr.

ROCKY MTN NAT'L PARK

8800

Colorado River

ARAPAHO NATIONAL RECREATION AREA

N

0   .5

Lake Granby

Granby Dam

Walden Hollow

Pumping Station

Colorado

Sunset Point

River

Cutthroat Bay Group Camp

Quinette Point

to Trail Ridge

P. 54

Stillwater Campground

8400

34

to Granby

Table Mtn 8830'

aquaduct

ARAPAHO NF

Willow

8400

8400

Creek

8400

ARAPAHO NRA

Willow Creek Reservoir

8800

Trail Mountain 9367'

8800

Arapaho Bay Campground: Tucked into the far southeast corner of the Lake Granby shoreline, this campground is a major gateway to the Indian Peaks Wilderness Area, a small though spectacular region of heavily glaciated mountains. The campground, built among mature lodgepole pines, offers shade in the summer but no grand vistas of either the lake or the mountains.

Lake Granby: The third and largest lake in a chain of reservoirs feeding the Alva B. Adams water diversion tunnel, Lake Granby forms the heart of the Arapaho National Recreation Area. Stocked with kokanee salmon and trout, the lake attracts osprey as well as fishermen.

Quinette Point Picnic Area: This small picnic area offers one of the best views of Lake Granby and the surrounding area. To the northwest looms the southern spur of the Never Summer Mountains. The Indian Peaks rise to the east. The Lake Granby Pumping Station stands directly across the water to the north. To the southeast, dikes hold back the waters of the lake.

Nature Note ■ Badgers: Largely uncelebrated, these compact, powerful weasels hunt mainly for ground squirrels in dry, open grasslands such as those west of Lake Granby. Their flat, heavy-boned bodies can squeeze into small burrows. Long claws on the forelimbs help them dig quickly, and short, shovel-like claws on the hind legs scoop away the loose dirt. These and other adaptations allow badgers to burrow faster than any other mammal. Badgers often prepare to dig out a ground squirrel burrow by plugging up all the exits so the squirrels can not escape. Besides ground squirrels, badgers eat pocket gophers, marmots, prairie dogs, birds' eggs, and carrion. ■

Willow Creek Reservoir: This small, serpentine lake nestles among rolling prairie foothills west of Lake Granby. Stands of lodgepole pine shade portions of the shoreline and groves of aspen trees rustle in the wind. Early and late in the day, mule deer emerge from the forest fringe to browse sagebrush and bitterbrush on the grassy hillsides. American kestrels, prairie falcons, northern harriers, and red-tailed hawks sweep the prairie, hunting for rodents.

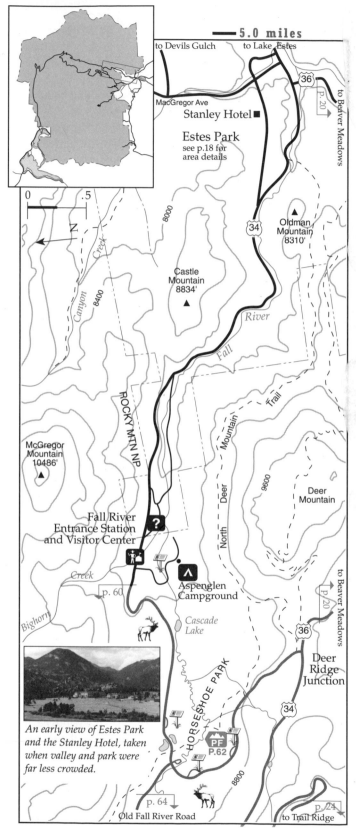

5.0 miles

to Devils Gulch   to Lake Estes

36

to Beaver Meadows

MacGregor Ave

Stanley Hotel ■

Estes Park
see p.18 for
area details

0   .5

Z

34

Oldman
Mountain
8310'

8000

Castle
Mountain
8834'
▲

Fall   River

ROCKY MTN NP

8400

McGregor
Mountain
10486'
▲

Trail

North   Deer   Mountain

9600

Deer
Mountain

Fall River
Entrance Station
and Visitor Center

?

p. 60

Creek

⚿ Aspenglen
Campground

to Beaver Meadows

p. 20

36

Bighorn

Cascade
Lake

HORSESHOE PARK

Deer
Ridge
Junction

*An early view of Estes Park
and the Stanley Hotel, taken
when valley and park were
far less crowded.*

P. 62

8800

34

p. 64

Old Fall River Road

p. 24

to Trail Ridge

US 34 (Eastside)

Stanley Hotel: This massive, five-story Victorian hotel overlooks the town of Estes Park and offers a terrific view of Longs Peak and its neighboring summits. The hotel was built in 1909 by Freelan Stanley, the wealthy inventor of an early photographic emulsion and the Stanley Steamer automobile. He had originally visited Estes Park in 1903 to recover from tuberculosis but grew to like the place and moved here.

Fall River Canyon: Between Estes Park and the border of Rocky Mountain National Park, the road twists and turns through a gorge cut into Precambrian granite by Fall River. The rocks are roughly 1.4 billion years old. The canyon—deep, narrow, and tortuous—is typical of a stream-eroded valley. Many of the park's valleys probably looked like it before immense glaciers gouged them into long, straight, steep-sided valleys. Those glaciers are thought to have advanced no lower than 8,000 feet in this region. As the road approaches the park, it climbs above the 8,000 foot mark, and the canyon opens into a spacious, glacially-carved valley.

Fall River Visitor Center: Exhibits in this recently-built visitor center cover the cycle of the park's seasons, profile some of its life communities, and display life-size bronzes of some of the park's most prominent animals. It also includes an interactive "Discovery Center" for kids.

Fall River Entrance Station: Monumental ponderosa pine spread their branches over the entrance station here and screen the edge of a long, open meadow. Like many of the meadows on the park's east side, this one was a lake bed plowed out by a glacier.

Aspenglen Campground: The short drive to the campground crosses Fall River and a tangle of dead trees, twisted metal, and boulders deposited here in July 1982 when a flash flood knocked out an old dam just above the campground. Two campers drowned. The flood began high above Horseshoe Park, where another old dam failed at Lawn Lake. Water filled Horseshoe Park, then roared down through Aspenglen Campground to Estes Park, where the torrent of water, mud, and debris reached a depth of 6 feet. For more on this flood, see pages 27, 63, and 65.

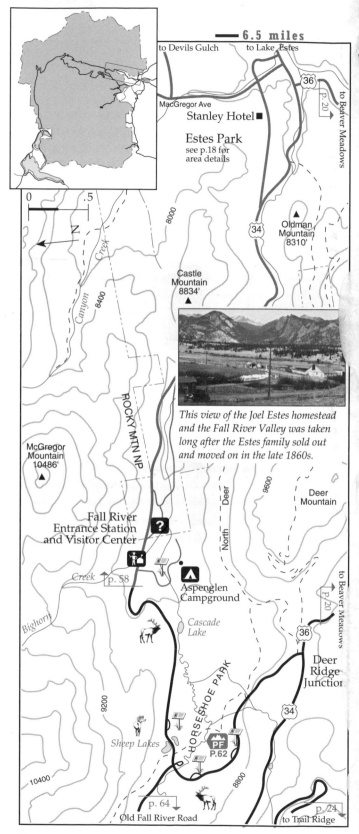

6.5 miles

to Devils Gulch   to Lake Estes

MacGregor Ave

Stanley Hotel ■

Estes Park
see p.18 for
area details

p. 20

to Beaver Meadows

36

34

▲ Oldman
Mountain
8310'

8000

Castle
Mountain
8834'
▲

0   .5

N

Canyon Creek

8400

*This view of the Joel Estes homestead
and the Fall River Valley was taken
long after the Estes family sold out
and moved on in the late 1860s.*

McGregor
Mountain
10486'
▲

ROCKY MTN NP

9600

Deer
Mountain

North Deer

**Fall River
Entrance Station
and Visitor Center** ?

p. 58

Creek

Bighorn

9200

▲ Aspenglen
Campground

*Cascade
Lake*

to Beaver Meadows

p. 20

36

**Deer
Ridge
Junction**

10400

Sheep Lakes

HORSESHOE PARK

P.62

34

8800

9200

p. 64
Old Fall River Road

p. 24
to Trail Ridge

Horseshoe Park: This expansive ponderosa parkland meadow has been filled by glaciers at least three times in the past 200,000 years. The distinct U-shaped track of glaciation is clearly visible in the forested notch at the head of the valley. After the last Pleistocene glacier retreated, a large lake spread over Horseshoe Park. The soils that eventually filled in the lake discourage tree growth because they are too fine-grained and too dry—except along Fall River, where they are too wet.

The meandering wetland river corridor, the abundance of grass, sedge, wildflowers, and browsable shrubs, as well as the protection offered by the surrounding forests of ponderosa pine and Douglas fir all draw a wide variety of animals to Horseshoe Park. You're likely to see bighorn sheep, elk, mule deer, coyotes, hawks, and songbirds.

The peaks of the Mummy Range stand roughly 4,300 feet above the floor of Horseshoe Park.

Sheep Lakes: Rangers sometimes stop traffic in Horseshoe Park so bighorn sheep can cross between Bighorn Mountain and the salt licks around Sheep Lakes. Roughly 650 bighorns roam the park in two flocks; one in the Mummy Range and one in the area of the Never Summer Mountains.

Bighorns gravitate toward the good forage available in open meadow areas, but rarely stray very far from the security of rocky ledges and rugged terrain. Every autumn, the bigger rams engage in spectacular head-smacking duels to determine who will breed with receptive ewes. The impact is so forceful that rams have evolved a shock-resistant double cranium.

Nature Note ■ The Divided Forest: Drought-resistant ponderosa pines grow widely spaced along the dry, south-facing slopes of Horseshoe Park. Directly across the valley, Douglas fir tends to predominate on the cooler, moister, north-facing slopes. ■

West Horseshoe Park: This parking area overlooks Fall River, a verdant riparian artery choked with shrub willow, thinleaf alder, water birch and mountain maple. Many types of small birds live among the thickets: robins, bluebirds, hummingbirds, warbling vireos, Swainson's thrushes, song sparrows, and Wilson's warblers.

From Horseshoe Park Overlook

Mt. Chapin
12,454 ft

Mount Chiquita
13,069 ft

Ypsilon Mtn.
13,514 ft

Fairchild Mtn.
13,502 ft

Bighorn Mtn.
11,463 ft

Exfoliation Dome

Dark Mtn.
10,859 ft

Alluvial Fan from
the 1982 flood

HORSESHOE PARK

Fall River

Reading the Landscape

■ **Mummy Range** ■ Glaciation left its mark on every peak in the Mummy Range visible from this point. Broad, U-shaped troughs form spacious valleys between Chapin and Chiquita and between Ypsilon and Fairchild. The upper end of a glacier gnawed into the east face of Ypsilon, leaving a rough, bowl-shaped hollow.

Ypsilon was named for Y-shaped fissures on its east face; Chapin for an 1880s Connecticut climber who wrote for magazines; Chiquita, perhaps, for the wife of the Ute Chief Ouray; and Fairchild for a Wisconsin politician.

■ **Sheep Lakes** ■ The small ponds are kettle lakes, which fill depressions formed by blocks of glacial ice once imbedded in the soil. When the ice chunks melted, they left potholes, which refill each year with rain and snowmelt.

■ **Alluvial Fan** ■ The heap of rubble spilling onto the valley floor west of Bighorn Mountain is an alluvial fan that formed during the flash flood of July 15, 1982. A dam built in 1903 at the foot of Lawn Lake, high in the Mummy Range, suddenly gave way, releasing 674 acre-feet of water into the steep Roaring River drainage. The wall of water ripped out trees, stripped the soil and sent 400-ton boulders tumbling down the canyon. Within an hour, debris that flushed down Roaring River had accumulated to a depth of 44 feet. The alluvium killed a hiker camped nearby and destroyed a lovely falls that used to spill into Horseshoe Park. It also dammed Fall River, creating a small lake, which is just out of view from this point. See also pages 27, 59, and 65.

■ **Exfoliation Domes** ■ Rounded, shield-like knobs of granite protrude from Bighorn Mountain and many other ridges and mountains on the park's east side. Granite expands slightly when relieved of overlying rock, creating a series of cracks or joints that parallel large, exposed surfaces. Water works into the joints and widens them by freezing. Eventually the freeze-thaw cycle sheers off a layer of curving slabs. Relieved of that load, the granite again expands slightly and creates a new series of joints.

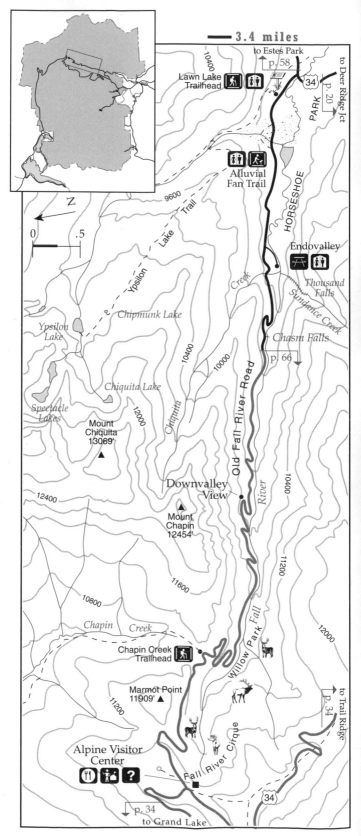

3.4 miles

to Estes Park
p. 58

to Deer Ridge Jct
p. 20

34

PARK

Lawn Lake Trailhead

HORSESHOE

Alluvial Fan Trail

Z

0   .5

10400

9600

Ypsilon Lake Trail

Endovalley

Thousand Falls

Sundance Creek

Chasm Falls

Chipmunk Lake

Ypsilon Lake

Chiquita Lake

Spectacle Lakes

Creek

10400

10000

p. 66

Old Fall River Road

River

Mount Chiquita 13069'

12000

Chiquita

Downvalley View

Mount Chapin 12454'

12400

10400

11200

Chapin   *Creek*

10800

11600

Chapin Creek Trailhead

Willow Park Fall

Marmot Point 11909' ▲

11200

to Trail Ridge
p. 34

12000

Alpine Visitor Center

Fall River Cirque

34

p. 34
to Grand Lake

64

Old Fall River Road

Lawn Lake Trailhead: From this vantage point under spreading ponderosa pines, the U-shaped track of the glacier that once filled Horseshoe Park is clearly visible at the foot of the Mummy Range. The trail climbs 6.2 miles along the steep Roaring River gorge, which was blasted clean of trees and soil by the flash flood of July 1982.

Alluvial Fan of the 1982 Flood: This inclined heap of rounded boulders is the most spectacular remaining evidence of the '82 Flood. When the dam failed, 674 acre feet of water slammed down the steep drainage of Roaring River, tearing out large trees, tossing boulders around like gumballs, and sweeping away the soil. It whipped down the gorge, rising to depths of 25 to 30 feet in the narrows, and cutting a gash as much as 50 feet into the ground. The swirling mass of water, mud, tree trunks, sand, and boulders crashed onto the floor of Horseshoe Park 45 minutes after the dam broke. Within an hour, the alluvium had piled up to a depth of 44 feet, damming Fall River and creating the small lake out on the valley floor.

An interpretive trail crosses the fan. Lodgepole pines, aspens, and various shrubs now grow among the rocks.

Old Fall River Road: This narrow, one-way gravel route was built by convict labor from 1913 to 1920. It climbs along the north wall of a deep, U-shaped valley carved out by the Fall River Glacier, which reached depths of 1,500 feet. The road passes through the montane, sub-alpine, and alpine tundra ecosystems, then joins Trail Ridge Road at the Alpine Visitor Center. A booklet from the roadside vending machine (also available at visitor centers) offers detailed, mile-by-mile commentary.

Chasm Falls: Here, Fall River zigzags through the forest and abruptly drops 25 feet through a narrow slot cut into the reddish-brown granite. This is a good place to look for water ouzels (also called American dippers). The small, gray bird is known for the quick, bobbing motion it performs as it pauses by the stream. Completely dependent on streams and rivers for food, the ouzel often wades with its head underwater, snatching up aquatic insects. It also strides across the streambed completely submerged and can dive to depths exceeding 20 feet.

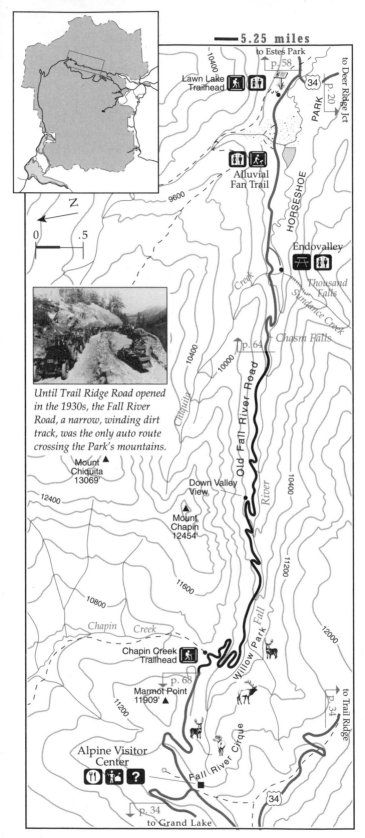

5.25 miles

to Estes Park
p. 58
PARK
to Deer Ridge Jct
p. 20
34

10400

Lawn Lake
Trailhead

HORSESHOE

9600

Alluvial
Fan Trail

Endovalley

*Thousand
Falls*

Sundance Creek

Chasm Falls

Creek

10400

10000

p. 64

Old Fall River Road

River

*Until Trail Ridge Road opened
in the 1930s, the Fall River
Road, a narrow, winding dirt
track, was the only auto route
crossing the Park's mountains.*

10400

Mount
Chiquita ▲
13069'

12400

Down Valley
View

Mount
Chapin ▲
12454'

Chiquita

11200

11600

Willow Park Fall

10800

Chapin   Creek

Chapin Creek
Trailhead

p. 68

Marmot Point
11909' ▲

11200

12000

to Trail
Ridge
p. 34

Alpine Visitor
Center

🍴 👥 ❓

Fall River Cirque

34

p. 34
to Grand Lake

N

0   .5

North of Chasm Falls: Within a mile of Chasm Falls, you enter the Subalpine Ecosystem, where dense ranks of subalpine fir and Engelmann spruce catch and hold vast quantities of snow each winter. The snow, the shade of the thick stands of trees, and the higher elevation combine to make this a cool, moist, dark environment.

Engelmann spruce have flakey bark and sharp, pointed needles. Subalpine fir have smooth, silvery bark and soft, flat needles. Limber pine, blue spruce, lodgepole, and aspen also grow here, but not in great numbers because they are not as well adapted to shade and cold.

Down Valley View: Just beyond a series of man-made rock terraces, called gabions, a hairpin turn opens up a magnificent vista of Fall River Canyon, Horseshoe Park, the small lake created by the 1982 flood, and the mountains above Estes Park. Here, too, you can get a clear sense of the depth and breadth of the Fall River Glacier by tracing the parabolic silhouette formed by the canyon walls.

Willow Park: This broad, subalpine meadow takes its name from knee-high thickets of shrub willow that serve as cover for rodents and birds. Grasses, sedges, and wildflowers also grow here, including golden banner, penstemon, fireweed, locoweed, elephant head, shooting stars, and dogtooth violets.

Elk and mule deer often feed in Willow Park. Clark's nutcrackers, Steller's jays, and hairy woodpeckers fly through the surrounding forest. Hawks and the occasional golden eagle glide overhead, looking for marmots and ground squirrels.

Beyond Willow Park: Above Willow Park, the road switchbacks through an old-growth forest of massive Engelmann spruce and subalpine fir. Some of these trees are more than 100 feet high, 400 years old, and have trunk diameters of three feet.

Beyond Chapin Creek Trailhead, these stately columns give way to isolated thickets of dwarf subalpine fir. Short, twisted, deformed, shrublike, seemingly half-dead, these tenacious little trees are often much older than trees ten times their height. Six-footers with three-inch trunks, for instance, can be more than 300 years old.

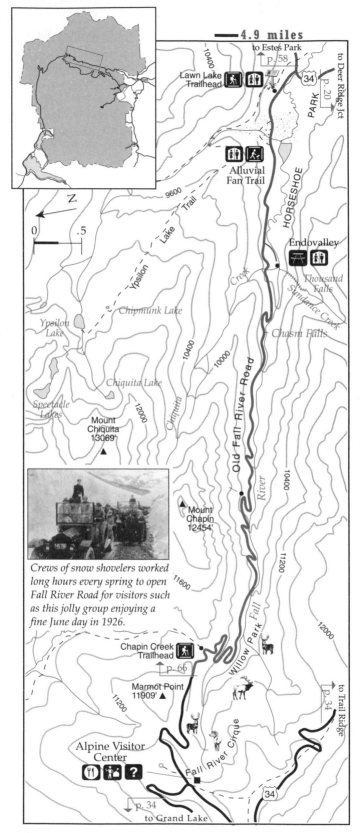

4.9 miles

to Estes Park

p. 58

to Deer Ridge Jct

34

p. 20

HORSESHOE PARK

Lawn Lake Trailhead

Alluvial Fan Trail

Endovalley

Thousand Falls

Sundance Creek

Chasm Falls

10400

9600

Ypsilon Lake Trail

Creek

Chipmunk Lake

Ypsilon Lake

10400

10000

Chiquita Lake

Chiquita

Old Fall River Road

Spectacle Lakes

12000

Mount Chiquita 13069'

▲ Mount Chapin 12454'

River

10400

11200

Crews of snow shovelers worked long hours every spring to open Fall River Road for visitors such as this jolly group enjoying a fine June day in 1926.

11600

Willow Park

Fall

Chapin Creek Trailhead

p. 66

Marmot Point 11909' ▲

11200

to Trail Ridge

p. 34

Fall River Cirque

12000

Alpine Visitor Center

34

p. 34

to Grand Lake

Z

0   .5

Fall River Cirque: The spacious, semi-circular dead end at the head of the valley is a cirque, the birthplace of Fall River Glacier. Steep walls curve down to a relatively flat floor, softened by mats of sedges, grasses, wildflowers, and thickets of low shrubs. Elk, mule deer, and bighorn sheep summer here.

Alpine Tundra: Treeless and at first glance barren, the alpine tundra is jammed with intriguing plants and animals that have adapted in fascinating ways to a bitterly cold, exceedingly dry, and wind-blasted climate. Plants arrange themselves in a complex patchwork of widely different communities that vary abruptly depending on soil conditions, wind exposure, and snow depth. For example, plants that have adapted to arid, desertlike conditions in gravelly soils may grow just a couple of feet from the rich soils of a sodden, alpine wetland.

Gopher Gardens: Aside from humans, no mammal exerts such a profound influence on tundra plant communities as the rat-sized pocket gopher. Its burrows criss-cross the surface of turf meadow and snowbed communities and can utterly change the character of the immediate landscape. As the gophers tunnel for tender shoots, they throw up sinuous mounds of soil that smother peripheral plants. Wind and water carry away topsoil, leaving a loose, gravelly soil soon colonized by bright, showy flowers that may not otherwise grow there: alpine aven, sky pilot, kings crown, yellow cinquefoil, and chiming bells. These distinct plant communities are called gopher gardens.

Nature Note ▪ Yellow-bellied Marmots: Closely related to groundhogs, yellow-bellied marmots live in meadows throughout the park but are especially conspicuous on the tundra. They dig burrow systems under and between boulders to avoid predators and hibernate as soon as they build up enough fat to last the winter (as early as August). In hibernation, their body temperatures plunge from 95 degrees to the low 40s; heart rates slow from 100 beats to 15; oxygen consumption falls to one-tenth the normal rate. Even at such a drastically reduced metabolic rate, marmots can lose between 30 percent and 50 percent of their body weight during the long winter. Look for them in the meadows and rock piles around the Alpine Visitor Center. ▪

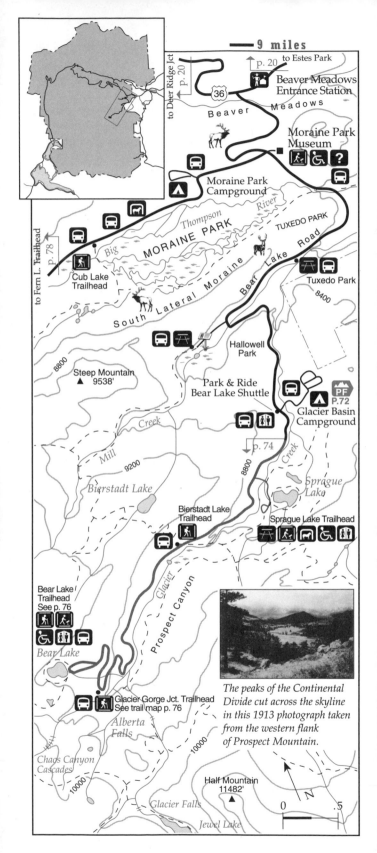

9 miles

to Estes Park

p. 20

to Deer Ridge Jct

36

Beaver Meadows Entrance Station

Beaver Meadows

Moraine Park Museum

?

Moraine Park Campground

Thompson River

MORAINE PARK

TUXEDO PARK

to Fern L. Trailhead

p. 78

Big

Cub Lake Trailhead

South Lateral Moraine

Bear Lake Road

Tuxedo Park

8400

Steep Mountain
▲ 9538'

Creek

Mill

9200

Bierstadt Lake

Hallowell Park

Park & Ride
Bear Lake Shuttle

p. 74

8800

Glacier Basin Campground

PF
P.72

Sprague Lake

Bierstadt Lake Trailhead

Sprague Lake Trailhead

Bear Lake Trailhead
See p. 76

Glacier

Creek

Prospect Canyon

The peaks of the Continental Divide cut across the skyline in this 1913 photograph taken from the western flank of Prospect Mountain.

Bear Lake

Glacier Gorge Jct. Trailhead
See trail map p. 76

Alberta Falls

Chaos Canyon Cascades

10000

Half Mountain
11482'
▲

N

0   .5

Glacier Falls

Jewel Lake

10000

Bear Lake Road

Beaver Meadows: Bear Lake Road crosses the eastern edge of Beaver Meadows, a spacious field of prairie grasses and wildflowers that sprawls at the foot of Trail Ridge. Cut by Beaver Brook, the meadow teems with rodents —mice, voles, shrews, ground squirrels, and pocket gophers. The rodents feast on seeds, roots, and berries, as well as on insects, especially grasshoppers.

Moraine Park: Separated from Beaver Meadows by a lateral moraine, Moraine Park is another expansive parkland meadow lying far below the peaks of the Front Range. With its interbraiding streams and its many beaver ponds, Moraine Park is much wetter than Beaver Meadows. Wet or not, it too supports a throng of rodents, which feed owls, hawks, coyotes, badgers and weasels.

Although a few elk feed in Moraine Park throughout the year, large herds congregate here for the annual ritual of autumn rut.

Tuxedo Park Picnic Area: Here amid the shade of immense ponderosa pines, crystalline Glacier Creek pours through great knobs and boulders of granite, gneiss, and schist. The rocks were deposited here as part of a lateral moraine by the Thompson Glacier, which plowed out Moraine Park. Some of the trees here and on the glacial outwash terrace downstream could be more than 300 years old. Clumps of common juniper grow among the picnic tables.

Glacier Basin Campground: Set in a forest of lodgepole pine, this beautiful campground offers the best roadside view of the peaks that make up the spectacular day-hiking country near Bear Lake. (See Peaks Finder, p. 72.)

Transportation Note ■ Park and Ride Shuttle Bus System: By mid-morning, parking areas jam at popular trailheads. To provide for the overflow, free buses depart from this point every 30 minutes during summer, with stops at Sprague Lake, Bierstadt Trailhead, Glacier Gorge Junction, and Bear Lake. The bus line links with another that runs the length of Moraine Park and extends up the Bear Lake Road to the Glacier Basin park-and-ride lot. During the summer of 2004, access to Bear Lake is by shuttle bus only, in order to accommodate road construction. ■

From Glacier Basin Campground

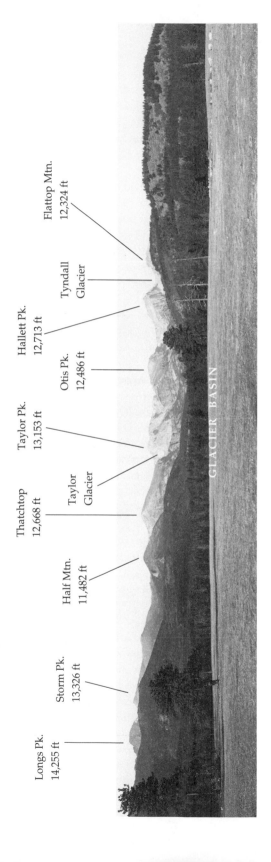

Longs Pk.
14,255 ft

Storm Pk.
13,326 ft

Half Mtn.
11,482 ft

Thatchtop
12,668 ft

Taylor
Glacier

Taylor Pk.
13,153 ft

Otis Pk.
12,486 ft

Hallett Pk.
12,713 ft

Tyndall
Glacier

Flattop Mtn.
12,324 ft

GLACIER BASIN

Reading the Landscape

■ A Hiker's Dream ■ Jutting high over dense forests of lodgepole pine and aspen, the rugged line of peaks visible from this point embraces the most popular hiking areas in the park. Every summer day, hundreds of climbers set out for the summit of Longs Peak. Many more tread the floor of aptly named Glacier Gorge, a deep furrow carved between Half and Thatchtop Mountains that ends at the nearly 4,000-vertical-foot west face of Longs Peak. Nearby, Loch Vale holds Glass Lake in a rocky grip below Taylor Peak, while Hallet Peak and Flattop Mountain rise above Bear Lake, Chaos Canyon, and Tyndall Gorge. (See trail map, p. 76.)

■ Ice Age Glaciers ■ During the ice ages, many small glaciers draped the crest of the peaks above Glacier Basin. At their upper ends, they carved out semi-circular hollows, called cirques. As they extended their reach downward, they widened existing stream courses into basins and spacious U-shaped valleys. Creeping down from almost every valley visible from this point, the individual fingers of ice converged to form a large valley glacier called the Bartholf Glacier. The ice advanced at least three times in the past several hundred thousand years, gnawing away at the cliffs, polishing the underlying rock surface and shoving millions of tons of boulders and other debris down the valley. Bierstadt Moraine, to the north, is a lateral moraine that formed beside Bartholf Glacier.

■ Glacier Basin ■ The flat meadow at your feet is a glacial outwash terrace. It's a mass of stratified sand and gravel deposited by interlacing streams of meltwater that drained the front of the Bartholf Glacier as it retreated for the last time. Water percolates quickly through such soils, which explains why few trees grow here.

■ Flat Summits ■ Geologists have puzzled for decades over the smooth, tilted surface of Hallett Peak and the even summits of Flattop Mountain, Otis Peak, and others. Untouched by Pleistocene glaciers, they represent an old erosional surface. The question is, how old? Some scientists have said hundreds of millions of years; others tens of millions. Current thinking interprets it as a five- to seven-million-year-old surface that was once continuous with the plains to the east.

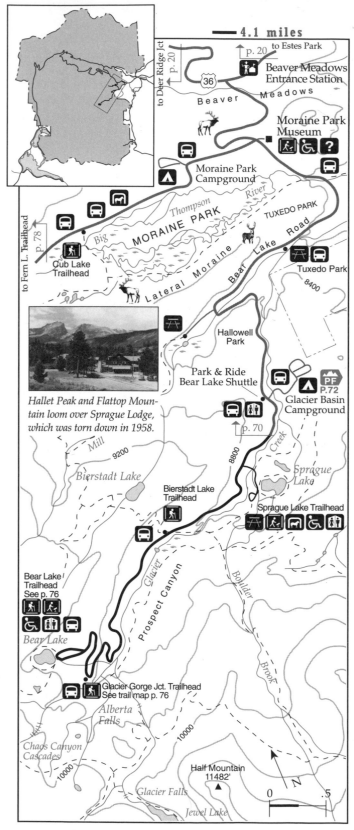

4.1 miles

to Estes Park

p. 20

Beaver Meadows
Entrance Station

to Deer Ridge Jct

36

Beaver Meadows

Moraine Park
Museum

?

Moraine Park
Campground

River

Thompson

MORAINE PARK

TUXEDO PARK

Bear Lake Road

Big

Lateral Moraine

Cub Lake
Trailhead

to Fern L. Trailhead

p. 78

8400

Tuxedo Park

Hallowell Park

Park & Ride
Bear Lake Shuttle

Glacier Basin
Campground

P.72

PF

Hallet Peak and Flattop Mountain loom over Sprague Lodge, which was torn down in 1958.

Mill

9200

Bierstadt Lake

p. 70

8800

Creek

Sprague
Lake

Bierstadt Lake
Trailhead

Sprague Lake Trailhead

Bear Lake
Trailhead
See p. 76

Glacier

Prospect Canyon

Boulder

Bear Lake

Glacier Gorge Jct. Trailhead
See trail map p. 76

Brook

Alberta
Falls

10000

Chaos Canyon
Cascades

10000

Half Mountain
11482'

N

Glacier Falls

0   .5

Jewel Lake

Sprague Lake: Abner Sprague built a resort lodge here in 1914 and dammed Glacier Creek to create a large trout pond for his guests. The lodge was torn down in 1958, but visitors still fish for trout. A nature trail suitable for wheelchairs and strollers loops around the water, offering reflected views of the peaks.

Bierstadt Lake Trailhead: The steep 1.4-mile trail scrambles up to Bierstadt Lake and a panorama of the peaks of the Continental Divide. The lake was named for the landscape artist Albert Bierstadt, who was hired by the Earl of Dunraven to paint scenes of the Estes Park area.

Prospect Canyon: Glacier Creek cut through layers of bedrock to create this narrow chasm, with its colorful rock walls and intimate streamside landscape. A miner built a cabin here in 1909 and prospected for seven years before throwing in the towel. Hence the name.

Nature Note ■ Forest Fire: In 1900, picnickers at Bear Lake touched off a forest fire that spread down the valley as far as Glacier Basin Campground and took months to extinguish. The flames destroyed a subalpine forest of Engelmann spruce, limber pine, and subalpine fir. Then lodgepole pine and aspen quickly pioneered the open areas, creating today's forest. In time, the subalpine species may regain the upper hand, but harsh winters slow the pace of forest succession. ■

Glacier Gorge Trailhead: Glacier Gorge is a broad, glaciated trough that runs along the west flank of Storm and Longs peaks. A series of small lakes and waterfalls attract hundreds of hikers daily. (See trail map p. 76.)

Bear Lake: Nestled beneath a ring of magnificent peaks, this small lake occupies a shallow depression carved out by glaciers and dammed by a large, lateral moraine. The ice, several hundred feet thick, spilled down from a trough between Flattop Mountain and Hallett Peak, which rise 3,000 feet above the water. A short trail circles the lake, and an accompanying brochure helps identify the trees, shrubs, birds, animals, and surrounding mountains. One conspicuous resident is the Clark's nutcracker, a raucous, crow-sized bird with black and white wings and a gray belly.

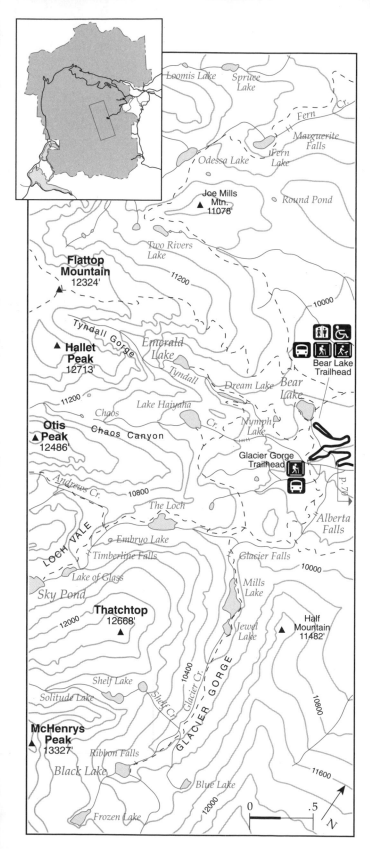

Bear Lake Area Trails

Emerald Lake: The walk to this small, glacial lake rises feet through a mixed forest of lodgepole, limber pine, and subalpine fir. First stop is Nymph Lake, with mats of yellow water lilies and reflected views of Hallett, Flattop, and Thatchtop. Between Nymph and Dream lakes, a terrific vista opens to Longs Peak and Glacier Gorge. Emerald Lake lies at tree limit, tucked into a cirque of 2,000-foot cliffs. Tyndall Glacier clings to the far wall. (Distance: 1.8 miles; elevation gain: 605 feet.)

Flattop Mountain: (Elev. 12,324 feet)A strenuous half day, this hike climbs far above tree limit and crosses the open tundra. It offers precipitous views of Dream and Emerald Lakes, top-of-the-world vistas of the surrounding peaks, and a chance to admire the tenacity of tiny alpine wildflowers. Not a good place to be caught in a lightning storm. (Distance one-way from Bear Lake: 4.4 miles; elevation gain: 2849 feet.)

Alberta Falls: Shaded by small aspen trees, this pleasant cascade pours over granite terraces smoothed and rounded by glaciers. The trip from Glacier Gorge Trailhead passes beaver dams and masses of wetland wildflowers. (Distance one-way: 0.6 miles; elevation gain: 160 feet.)

Loch Vale and Sky Pond: A leisurely, full-day hike, this route climbs past Alberta Falls and follows a spacious, glaciated valley along the northwest flank of Thatchtop. Spectacular cliffs soar 1,000 feet above The Loch, a beautiful glacial tarn surrounded by boulders and limber pines. A short sidetrip leads to Timberline Falls, one of the loveliest cascades in the park. Lake of Glass and Sky Pond both lie in a dramatic basin covered with alpine tundra and bounded by 2,200-foot cliffs. (Distance one-way: 4.6 miles; elevation gain: 1660 feet.)

Glacier Gorge to Black Lake: This huge glacial trough stretches from the base of Longs Peak to Glacier Falls and embraces some of the most beautiful lakes in the park. From Mills Lake onward, you walk beneath a vast, continuous wall of rock that curves for miles along the left side of the gorge and sweeps upward 4,300 feet to the summit of Longs Peak. Black Lake lies at the head of the gorge, ringed by 2,500-foot cliffs. (Distance one-way: 4.7 miles; elevation gain: 1390 feet.)

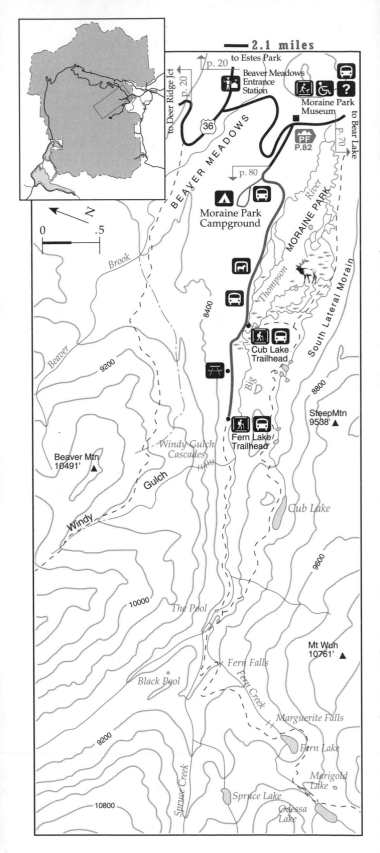

2.1 miles

to Estes Park

Beaver Meadows
Entrance
Station

to Deer Ridge Jct

p. 20

p. 20

Moraine Park
Museum

to Bear Lake

36

BEAVER MEADOWS

PF

P.82

p. 80

P. 70

Moraine Park
Campground

MORAINE PARK

Thompson River

N

0   .5

Brook

8400

Beaver

9200

South Lateral Moraine

Cub Lake
Trailhead

Big

8800

Windy Gulch
Cascades

Fern Lake
Trailhead

SteepMtn
9538'

Gulch

Beaver Mtn
10491'

Windy

Cub Lake

9600

10000

The Pool

Mt Wuh
10761'

Fern Falls

Black Pool

Fern Creek

Marguerite Falls

9200

Fern Lake

Spruce Creek

Marigold
Lake

Spruce Lake

Odessa
Lake

10800

Moraine Park

Moraine Park Museum: Exhibits in this terrific museum describe the creation of the park's landscape, from the formation of Precambrian metamorphic rock to the uplift and glaciation of the Front Range. The exhibits specifically tailor their lessons to the valley you see from the museum's windows. Other displays summarize major ecosystems in the park, and a nature trail acquaints visitors with wildflowers often found in parkland meadows.

Moraine Park: Moraine Park typifies the rolling, savanna-like parkland habitat that occupies much of Rocky Mountain's eastern foothills. Along the south-facing slopes, huge ponderosa pines spread over an expansive understory of grasses, sun sedge, shrubs, and prairie wildflowers. Douglas fir grow along the cooler, wetter, north-facing slopes, and aspen groves occupy moist swales and ravines.

Birds are abundant here: Steller's jays, nuthatches, hairy woodpeckers, ravens, chickadees, juncos, pine siskins, and yellow-rumped warblers. Predatory birds include great horned owls, goshawks, and red-tailed hawks.

Roadside Pines: Large ponderosa pines grow along the road and and dot the south-facing slopes of the Moraine Park. Ponderosas are the largest conifers in the Southern Rockies, reaching heights of 150 feet with trunk diameters of 3 to 4 feet. Ponderosa needles are four to seven inches long and grow in bunches of three. Their thick, platey bark protects them from grass fires. Creases in the bark smell like vanilla, butterscotch, or pineapple. Ponderosas prefer a hot, dry climate and collect water through a taproot and a wide radius of lateral roots. They do not tolerate shade very well and often yield ground to Douglas-fir trees where the two species grow together.

Abert's Squirrel ▪ These dark-furred, tassel-eared squirrels depend almost exclusively on ponderosa pines for food, cover, and nesting sites. Much larger and quieter than the red squirrel of the Douglas-fir forest, Abert's squirrels feed on ponderosa cones and the inner bark of ponderosa twigs. They show a marked preference for feeding from trees that have smaller amounts of aromatic chemicals in the sap. ▪

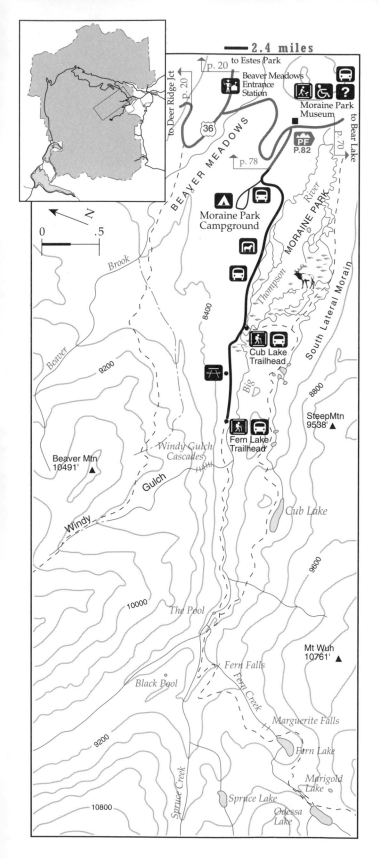

Big Thompson River: Between Moraine Park Campground and Cub Lake Trailhead, the road parallels the Big Thompson River, which soaks a broad section of the valley floor. In this intricate wetland setting, shrubs such as willows, alder, mountain maple, and river birch form a nearly continuous corridor of thickets, which opens occasionally to reveal an achingly beautiful bend of the river, or a beaver pond. The river banks brim with forbs, grasses, sedges, rushes, climbing vines, and many wildflowers. Songbirds hop from perch to perch among the shrubs. Muskrats grub among aquatic plants for roots, tubers, and stems.

Named for the belt of blue-gray feathers across their white breasts, these long-billed, large-headed belted kingfishers dive after fish in the ponds and pools by the road. They usually build their nests in burrows they dig into the banks of the river. Parents teach young to fish by dropping dead meals into the water for retrieval.

Cub Lake Trail: This 2.8-mile trail crosses the marshy upper end of Moraine Park and climbs 540 feet to a small, shallow lake rich in yellow pond lilies.

Aspen Groves: The road passes through a thick grove of aspens as it approaches Fern Lake Trailhead. Most of the tree trunks have been chewed by wintering elk and mule deer, which accounts for the black and white patterns on the bark that resemble leopard spots.

Fern Lake Trail: You'll find a curiously diverse mix of trees and plants near the trailhead. Moisture-loving aspens, cottonwoods and, of course, ferns grow near ponderosas, which like it dry, hot, and sunny. And the ponderosas grow close to spruce, Douglas fir, and western red cedar, which like it cool, damp, and shady. The diversity of plant species reflects a variety of microclimates crushed benevolently into the upper end of the valley. The wetland corridor of the Big Thompson River; the dry, sunny, south-facing slopes; the channel of cold air that funnels down from the mountains at night—all these factors provide different growing conditions.

The trail climbs 1,375 feet over 3.8 miles to Fern Lake, offering views of Notchtop and Stones Peak.

From Moraine Park Museum

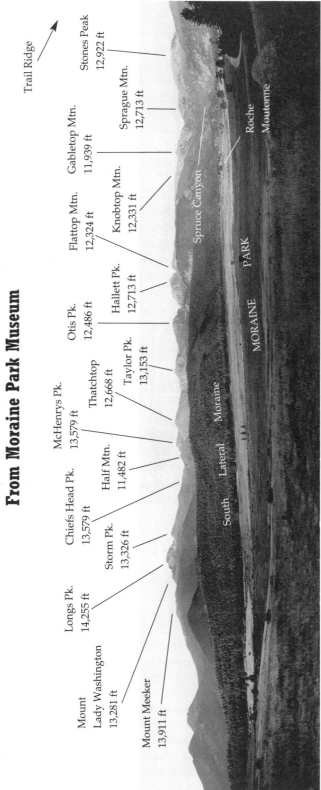

Trail Ridge

Stones Peak
12,922 ft

Sprague Mtn.
12,713 ft

Gabletop Mtn.
11,939 ft

Flattop Mtn.
12,324 ft

Knobtop Mtn.
12,331 ft

Otis Pk.
12,486 ft

Hallett Pk.
12,713 ft

McHenrys Pk.
13,579 ft

Thatchtop
12,668 ft

Taylor Pk.
13,153 ft

Chiefs Head Pk.
13,579 ft

Half Mtn.
11,482 ft

Storm Pk.
13,326 ft

Longs Pk.
14,255 ft

Mount
Lady Washington
13,281 ft

Mount Meeker
13,911 ft

Spruce Canyon

Roche
Moutonne

MORAINE

PARK

South

Lateral

Moraine

Reading the Landscape

■ **Moraine Park** ■ This broad, flat-floored valley once lay beneath the lower end of the great Thompson Glacier, which extended from Moraine Park far beyond Stones Peak and filled Forest Canyon to a depth of 2,000 to 2,500 feet. It left a depression and the leading edge of the glacier—a terminal moraine—dammed the Big Thompson River and created a lake. The lake then filled in with sand, mud, silt, and decomposed plants to form the nearly level surface of Moraine Park.

■ **Lateral Moraines** ■ The long, forested ridge across the valley is South Lateral Moraine—a heap of rubble that piled up along the sides of Thompson Glacier and was then overgrown with trees. The Moraine Park road runs along a corresponding lateral moraine on the north side of the valley.

■ **Roche Moutonne** ■ Thompson Glacier flowed over and around this smooth hump of resistant rock that rises in the center of the valley like a small island. One of several in Rocky Mountain National Park, such landforms were given their French name by an imaginative Swiss man in 1787 who thought the ones he saw in the Alps looked like wigs greased with mutton fat. Over 200 years later, who can dispute the resemblance?

■ **Erratics** ■ Large boulders scattered here and there on the floor of Moraine Park are called erratics. They were plucked out of the high cliffs and transported here in the frozen mass of Thompson Glacier. When the ice melted, they were left behind.

■ **The Mountains** ■ Longs Peak, its neighboring summits, and other mountains along the Continental Divide rise more than 5,000 feet over the floor of Moraine Park. Composed of Precambrian granite, gneiss, and schist, the mountain core rose along fault zones 60 to 70 million years ago.

The small glaciers found toward the crest of the range are not remnants of the Pleistocene glaciers that carved the many cirques, bowls, and U-shaped valleys visible from this point. Instead, today's glaciers began forming several thousand years ago and have retreated in recent decades. Remnants of five active glaciers still exist within the park.

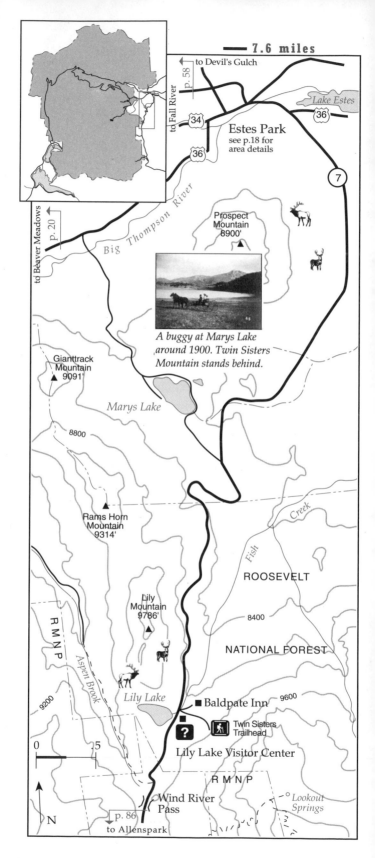

7.6 miles

to Devil's Gulch
p. 58

Lake Estes

to Fall River

34   36

Estes Park
see p.18 for
area details

7

to Beaver Meadows
p. 20

Big Thompson River

Prospect
Mountain
8900'

A buggy at Marys Lake around 1900. Twin Sisters Mountain stands behind.

Gianttrack
Mountain
9091'

Marys Lake

8800

Rams Horn
Mountain
9314'

Fish Creek

ROOSEVELT

Lily
Mountain
9786'

8400

NATIONAL FOREST

R M N P

Aspen Brook

9200

Lily Lake

■ Baldpate Inn

9600

?

🚶 Twin Sisters
Trailhead

Lily Lake Visitor Center

0   5

R M N P

N

**Wind River
Pass**

p. 86
to Allenspark

*Lookout
Springs*

84

Colorado Highway 7

Marys Lake: Nestled into a rolling, parkland meadow dotted with ponderosa pines and bulbous knobs of granite, Marys Lake is a reservoir in the Colorado–Big Thompson Water Diversion Project. Much of the lake's water comes from the west slope of the Front Range by way of a 13-mile tunnel bored through the mountains during the 1940s. The tunnel carries water to East Portal, at the end of Colo. 66, then a siphon and another tunnel carry it to Marys Lake. From here, it enters a third tunnel, through Prospect Mountain, and flows to Lake Estes. Power plants at Marys Lake and Estes Park run the water through turbines to generate electricity.

Fish Creek Canyon: The road climbs about 1,500 feet above Estes Park, snaking along the west wall of Fish Creek Canyon. The granite, gneiss, and schist that compose the cliffs are 1.4 to 1.7 billion years old and are the same rocks that form the core of the Front Range. The open meadows in the valley below are winter range for elk and mule deer. Years ago, bison and bighorn sheep also wintered there. Bison have vanished from the region and sheep, although present elsewhere in the park, haven't used this range for many years.

Baldpate Inn: Perched on the rim of Fish Creek Canyon, this historic timber frame lodge overlooks Estes Park and offers terrific views from its verandah of Estes Cone, Longs Peak, and Mount Lady Washington.

Lily Lake: Early residents of the valley often saw wolves and bighorn sheep beside this lake, which was named for the abundant water lilies that once covered its surface. Wolves were exterminated long ago, and the lilies drowned after the lake was made into a reservoir and the water level rose. Deer and elk still feed along its shore, and trout dapple its surface on quiet evenings. The meadows around the lake are good places to look for prairie wildflowers such as paintbrush, asters, shrubby cinquefoil, yarrow, lupine, and gilia.

Paintbrush is a semi-parasite and produces only a fraction of the food it needs. Instead, it steals nutrients from the roots of neighboring plants, often sagebrush.

Modest exhibits at the visitor center across the road offer a primer on the area's plants and animals.

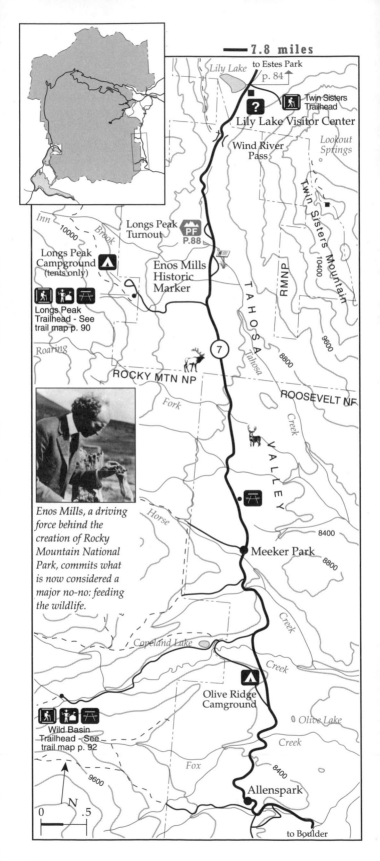

7.8 miles

to Estes Park
p. 84

Lily Lake

Twin Sisters Trailhead

Lily Lake Visitor Center

Wind River Pass

Lookout Springs

Longs Peak Turnout
PF **P.88**

Enos Mills Historic Marker

Longs Peak Campground (tents only)

Longs Peak Trailhead - See trail map p. 90

Roaring

Inn

Brook

TAHOSA

RMNP

Twin Sisters Mountain

7

ROCKY MTN NP

Fork

ROOSEVELT NF

Tahosa

V A L L E Y

Creek

8800

8400

Meeker Park

8800

Horse

Enos Mills, a driving force behind the creation of Rocky Mountain National Park, commits what is now considered a major no-no: feeding the wildlife.

Copeland Lake

Creek

Creek

Olive Ridge Camground

Olive Lake

Wild Basin Trailhead - See trail map p. 92

Fox

Creek

8400

Allenspark

N

0   .5

to Boulder

86

Tahosa Valley: This broad, rolling valley between Longs Peak and Twin Sisters Mountain formed along a fault line. Ponderosa pine and lodgepole pine forests start at the edge of the valley floor, providing cover for the elk and mule deer who forage among the grasses and shrubs at dawn and dusk.

Tahosa is a Kiowa word meaning "Top of the Mountains," or "Dwellers of the Mountaintops." The valley was a base of operations for some of the early resorts, including Longs Peak Inn, which was run by Enos Mills, the park's founding father.

Longs Peak Turnout: Views of Longs Peak don't get better than this unless you hike into the backcountry. The summit was named for a young Army officer, Stephen Harrison Long, who traversed the base of the Front Range in 1820.

The park's highest peak (14,255 feet), it bears the scars of glaciation on every flank. Its East Face, which overlooks the Tahosa Valley, is a glacial cirque with dramatic walls soaring roughly 2,000 feet above appropriately named Chasm Lake.

One of the cliffs, a broad sheet of smooth rock called The Diamond, rises continuously for 1,000 feet and is considered one of the most challenging technical climbs in Colorado. (See Peaks Finder, p. 88.)

Enos Mills Historic Marker: Enos Mills built the small log cabin across the meadow from this marker in 1885, when he was just 15 years old. He had come to Colorado from Kansas in precarious health, but thrived here. He worked as a cowboy and miner, then climbing guide, innkeeper, author, naturalist, and conservationist.

He wrote lyrically and intelligently about the natural world and, in 1909, proposed creating a national park that would extend from Estes Park clear to Pikes Peak, near Colorado Springs.

Teddy Roosevelt supported the idea for a national park and encouraged Mills to stump for it. Mills and other supporters spent the next six years doing just that. In 1915, Rocky Mountain National Park was dedicated, though on a scale much reduced from Mills' original vision.

Mills died in 1922. The homestead cabin (stuffed with Mills memorabilia) is still opened for tours during the summer.

From Longs Peak Turnout

Mount Meeker
13,911 ft

Mills Glacier

Longs Peak
14,255 ft

Mount Lady Washington
13,281 ft

Reading the Landscape

■ **Longs Peak** ■ After his own attempt to scale
Longs Peak failed in 1864, William Beyers, editor
of the *Rocky Mountain News*, predicted that no one
"will ever be upon its summit." His prediction came
a bit late. Arapaho had been climbing to the summit
for decades, perhaps centuries. There, they built
stone blinds, covered them with sticks, and baited
eagles with carrion. When an eagle landed, they
grabbed it through the roof, plucked a few feathers,
and let it go.

Four years after making his prediction, Beyers
reached the summit with John Wesley Powell, the one-
armed geology professor who launched his famous
exploration of the Grand Canyon the same year. Soon,
the ascent became routine. Today, hundreds of hikers
set out for the summit daily. (See Longs Peak trail
map, p 90.)

The summit, composed mainly of granite 1.4 billion years old, rises about 5,100 feet from the valley
floor. It stands so far above tree limit that even the
tenacious plants of the alpine tundra give out. Little
more than lichens grow above 14,000 feet, where
winter winds gust to 200 mph.

■ **Mount Meeker** ■ The park's second-highest peak
(13,911 feet) was named for Nathan Meeker, a rigid,
idealistic agriculture editor of the *New York Tribune*
who in 1870 founded an experimental farming colony
on the Colorado plains—Greeley. Meeker later became
Indian agent for the Ute reservation in western Colorado. He tried to coerce the tribe into farming, was
bitterly resented for his attempt, and then killed in
1879 when he dug an irrigation ditch across a field
where the Ute raced horses.

■ **Hawks & Owls** ■ Rodents and rabbits abound in the
grassy meadows that stretch across the floor of Tahosa
Valley, and so do their avian predators. The better to
see their prey, hawks have evolved eyes that function
very much like telescopes, delivering a large-scale,
high-resolution image. Nocturnal owls rely more on a
keen sense of hearing. Some are capable of catching
prey by sound alone. Owls also have the advantage of
stealth. They fly silently, thanks to specially adapted
feathers on the leading edge of their wings that
eliminate the vortex noise created by airflow over a
smooth surface.

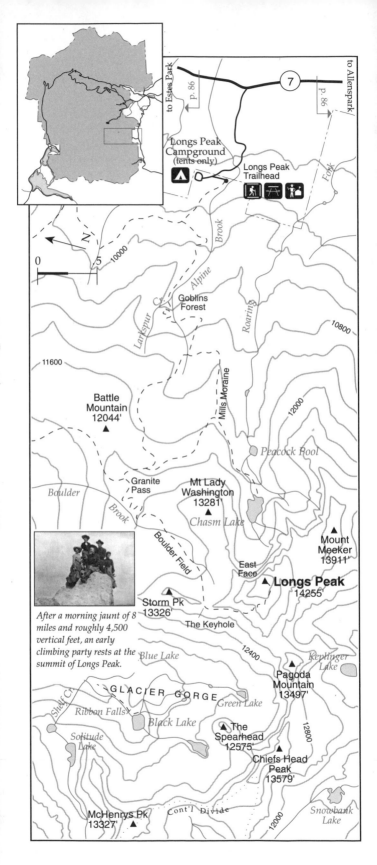

Longs Peak Area Trails

Longs Peak—The Route: Climbers have recorded more than a hundred separate routes to the summit of Longs Peak, but most people follow the **East Longs Peak Trail,** which starts at the Longs Peak Ranger Station.

Though the route is a "walk-up," and even though some 10,000 people tread the summit each summer, the trip should never be undertaken lightly. The 8-mile ascent climbs 4,855 feet and usually takes seven to eight hours. The return trip usually lasts about five footsore hours. Because thunderstorms often form by early afternoon, hikers are advised to reach the summit by noon and start their descent long before the lightning bolts start dancing on the treeless surface. No water along the trail should be drunk without treating it or boiling it. Conditions can change quickly, so hikers should pack for sleet, snow, wind, heat, and intense sunlight.

The trail first traverses the eastern flank of **Battle Mountain** passing through lodgepole pines and into limber pines at Goblins Forest (1.2 miles). Engelmann spruce and subalpine fir predominate to tree limit, reached at roughly 10,500 feet, as the path zigzags along Mills Moraine. This lateral moraine was piled up by the same glacier that carved out the East Face of Longs Peak. A spur trail branches off to **Chasm Lake** (less than a mile's walk). Near the junction you get a terrific view of Peacock Pool, a sapphire gem of water cradled far below in the glacial trough bounded by Mills Moraine.

From the junction, the Longs Peak route heads north and circles the base of Mount Lady Washington, passing stony tracts of vivid alpine wildflowers.

At **Granite Pass** (3.7 miles), the route turns southwest and scrambles across the Boulder Field to the Keyhole, a gap in the ridge between Storm and Longs Peak. From here, the route traverses the West Face, offering spectacular views of Glacier Gorge, and then ascends a steep ramp of granite that ends on the flat, roomy summit. The route from the **Keyhole** to the summit, marked by dots painted on the rocks, requires rock scrambling and often takes a couple of hours.

On the summit, you can gaze down the East Face to Chasm Lake, 2,500 feet below, pick out Wyoming's Medicine Bow Mountains, glance across the Great Plains, and trace the spine of the Rockies south for dozens of miles.

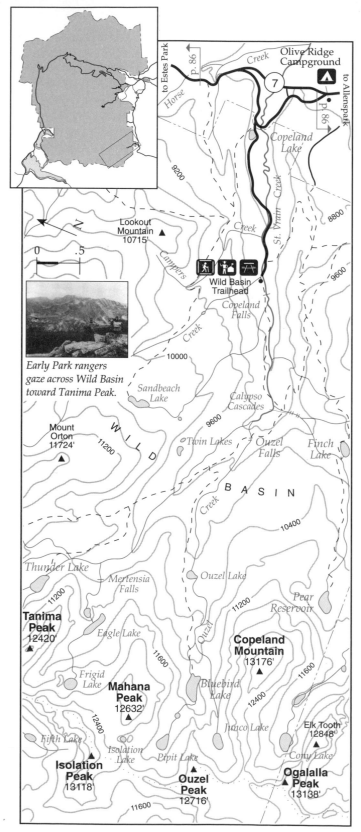

to Estes Park

Horse Creek

Olive Ridge Campground

7

to Allenspark

P. 86

P. 86

Copeland Lake

St. Vrain Creek

9200

8800

9600

Lookout Mountain
10715'

Creek

Campers

Wild Basin Trailhead

Copeland Falls

Early Park rangers gaze across Wild Basin toward Tanima Peak.

N

0   .5

10000

Creek

Sandbeach Lake

Calypso Cascades

9600

W   I   L   D

Mount Orton
11724'

Twin Lakes

Ouzel Falls

Finch Lake

11200

B   A   S   I   N

Creek

10400

Thunder Lake

Mertensia Falls

Ouzel Lake

Pear Reservoir

11200

Tanima Peak
12420'

Eagle Lake

11200

Ouzel

Copeland Mountain
13176'

11600

Frigid Lake

Mahana Peak
12632'

Bluebird Lake

12400

11600

Fifth Lake

Junco Lake

Elk Tooth
12848'

12400

Isolation Lake

Pipit Lake

Cony Lake

Isolation Peak
13118'

Ouzel Peak
12716'

Ogalalla Peak
13138'

11600

92

Wild Basin Area Trails

Wild Basin: West of Meeker Park, this spacious valley was
hollowed out during the ice ages by a large glacier
with tributaries that reached high into the crest of the
range all the way from Mount Meeker south to
Copeland Mountain. The glacier formed and advanced
at least three times, and its foot once extended east of
the highway. Like so many glaciated regions, Wild
Basin is a footloose joy. Small lakes nestle into rock-
walled cirques. Dense subalpine forests cloak the
mountain slopes and give way to spongy subalpine
meadows thick with wildflowers. Icy streams tumble
from the cliffs as lovely cascades and snake through
the trees and meadows.

Ouzel Falls: (Elev. 9450 feet) The trail starts beyond
Copeland Lake (with its fine view of Copeland Mountain) at the Wild Basin Ranger Station. It follows
North St. Vrain Creek past Copeland Falls and then
climbs through a forest of subalpine fir and Engelmann spruce to Calypso Cascades, named for the
calypso orchids, or fairy slippers, that bloom nearby
in July. The trail traverses the valley wall through
several areas burned by a 1978 wildfire before arriv-
ing at the falls named by Enos Mills for the chunky
water ouzel.

Bluebird Lake: (Elev. 10,978 feet) Roughly a half mile
beyond Ouzel Falls, a 2.7-mile spur trail climbs
toward Bluebird Lake, which is surrounded by
bare rock outcroppings and ringed by the cliffs of
Copeland Mountain, Ouzel Peak, and Mahana Peak.
The trail passes through an area cleared of trees by
the 1978 wildfire, rises past Ouzel Lake, and wanders
among subalpine forests and meadows before reaching the lake.

Thunder Lake: (Elev. 10,574 feet) This beautiful glacial lake
lies beneath a forested slope with excellent views of
Mount Alice, Tanima Peak, Pagoda Mountain, and
Longs Peak. The trail continues 2.7 miles beyond the
Bluebird Lake turnoff, switchbacking through limber
pines and curving under the shade of Engelmann
spruce and subalpine fir. The meadows around the
lake are stuffed with wildflowers: lousewort, marsh
marigold, mountain bluebell, penstemon, elephant
head, and bistort. The 1930s cabin located at Thunder
Lake is one several from this period in the Park.

Index

Further Reading

Arno & Hammerly. *Northwest Trees*. The Mountaineers, Seattle, WA, 1977.

Arps and Kingery. *High Country Names: Rocky Mountain National Park and Indian Peaks*. Johnson Publishing Company, Inc., Boulder, CO, 1977, 1994.

Benyus, Janine M. *The Field Guide to Wildlife Habitats of the Western United States*. Simon & Schuster Inc., New York, NY, 1989.

Buchholtz, C W. *Rocky Mountain National Park: A History*. Colorado Associated University Press, Boulder, CO, 1983.

Dannen, Kent & Donna. *Hiking Rocky Mountain National Park*. The Globe Pequot Press, Old Saybrook, CT, 2002.

Ehrlich, Dobkin & Wheye. *The Birder's Handbook*. Simon & Schuster, New York, NY, 1988.

Peattie, Donald Culross. *A Natural History of Western Trees*. Houghton Mifflin Co., Boston, 1950; reissued 1991.

Robertson, Leigh. *Southern Rocky Mountain Wildflowers*. Falcon Publishing Company, Helena, MT. 1999.

Roederer, Scott. *Birding Rocky Mountain National Park*. Johnson Books, 2002.

Schmidt, Jeremy. *Adventuring in the Rockies: A Travel Guide to the Rocky Mountain Regions of Canada and the U.S.A.* Sierra Club Books, San Francisco, 1986, 1994.

Shattil, Rozinski & Titlow. *Rocky Mountain National Park: Beyond Trail Ridge*. Westcliffe Publishers, Inc., Englewood, CO, 1986.

Smith, Wendy et alia. *Field Guide to Wildlife Viewing in Rocky Mountain National Park*. Rocky Mountain Nature Assn.

Willard & Foster. *A Roadside Guide to Rocky Mountain National Park*. Johnson Publishing Company, Inc., Boulder, CO, 1990.

Zwinger & Willard. *Land Above the Trees*. The University of Arizona Press, Tucson, AZ, 1972.

Thomas Schmidt fell for the Rocky Mountains as a boy, while spending summers in the West with his family.

He is the author of four books about the human and natural history of the West and has contributed to many other books published by the National Geographic Society.

He lives in Bozeman, Montana, with his wife, Terese, and their two children, Pat and Colleen.

Wendy Baylor and Jeremy Schmidt,
  Computer composition and design for original edition

Wendy Baylor, *Maps*

National Park Service, *Historic photos*

Jocelyn Slack, *Illustrations*

National Geographic Travel Books:

Caroline Hickey, *Project Manager*

Cinda Rose, *Art Director*

Bea Jackson, *Cover Design*

Library of Congress Cataloging-in-Publication Data

Schmidt, Thomas, 1959-
  National Geographic Rocky Mountain National Park road guide:
  the essential guide for motorists / by Thomas Schmidt.
    p. cm.
Includes index.
  ISBN 0-7922-6641-2
1. Rocky Mountain National Park (Colo.)--Guidebooks.
2. Automobile travel--Colorado--Rocky Mountain National
Park--Guidebooks.
I. Title: Rocky Mountain National Park road guide. II. National
Geographic Society
(U.S.) III. Title.

F782.R59S36 2004

917.88'6904--dc22   2003022224